THE ODYSSEY
AND DR. NOVAK

THE ODYSSEY
AND DR. NOVAK

A MEMOIR

Ann C. Colley

SHE WRITES PRESS

Published May 22, 2018
Printed in the United States of America
Print ISBN: 978-1-63152-343-4
E-ISBN: 978-1-63152-344-1
Library of Congress Control Number: 2017955635

Interior design by Tabitha Lahr

For information, address:
She Writes Press
1563 Solano Ave #546
Berkeley, CA 94707

She Writes Press is a division of SparkPoint Studio, LLC.

Names and identifying characteristics have been changed to
protect the privacy of certain individuals.

To Alice and Herbert Rowe

CONTENTS

INTRODUCTION:

The Odyssey

> *Sing to me of the person, Muse, the person of twists*
> *and turns, who through the touch of a hand is fated*
> *to travel from her native land over the boundless*
> *earth and across the rush of gusting winds into*
> *regions where she knows not the language nor the*
> *way of life.*
> —Adapted from Book I of *The Odyssey*

Looking out of the plane's window at the endlessly starry skies, like Telemachus, I wonder what has possessed me. It is late August 1995. Having abandoned the familiar routines of my life in Buffalo, I am on my way to Poland where for the coming year I shall lecture in English at the University of Warsaw. All night long, wrapped in a fleece, when not surrendering to the enticing oblivion of sleep, I weigh my chosen course and occasionally assuage my anxiety by leafing through a pamphlet on Polish etiquette. Did you know that in polite Polish society, it is thought improper for a woman to walk down the street with her hands in her pockets?

Knowing scarcely any Polish after a prefatory two-week language course that has taught me little beyond how to utter a greeting and how to ask the way, I worry about how I am to make sense of my new surroundings. Condemned to chart my course through either the veil of translation or the hesitating guidance of a nonverbal gesture, such as a telling, subtle turn of a hand, I long for a "bright-eyed Athena," to reassure me that "some of the words you'll find within yourself, / the rest some power will inspire you to say" (*The Odyssey*). Irving Massey, my multilingual partner, is not to join me for another month.

Five years pass, and again I leave the customary rhythms and language of Buffalo to embark on a year's journey to Ukraine, a country that initially is even less familiar to me than Poland had been. I am to join the Foreign Literature Department at Taras Shevchenko University in Kiev. This time I have received no language instruction at all. To make matters worse, I have no practice in reading the Cyrillic alphabet. As a result, worry and discomfort are once more my traveling companions, but, as before, they do not conspire, like Aeolus, to blow me off course and tear to shreds the sails of my curiosity and wreck my desire to be there. My insecurities might loose the sack and let all the winds burst out, but I grit my teeth and hold firm to my lifelong fascination with that part of the world. Ever since childhood Central and Eastern Europe have intrigued, if not bewitched, me. Not possessing the ability to enter these cultures through the sounds and words of their language, I must tread the land and see things for myself.

What follows is a composite portrait of Poland in 1995 and Ukraine in 2000. During these years, both countries are, in their own ways, not only still dominated by the shadows of their pasts (their remembrances of war and the Holocaust) but also suspended between one mode of life and another. Having gained relative autonomy after the collapse of the Soviet Union in 1991, each is trying to chart its course. Caught between its old loyalties to Soviet rule and its increasing devotion to a Westernized economy, Poland is unsettled yet gradually realizing its entrepreneurial dreams. Ukraine, on the other hand, contends with its continuing dependency upon Russia as well as with its own internal quarrels. In spite of these tensions, in 2000, many Ukrainians are optimistically working toward forming more active connections with the West. They have hopes of joining the European Union. Few are yet explicitly imagining the deadly insanity of open civil conflict between Ukrainian nationalists and pro-Russian separatists. Nor are they expecting that, in just over a decade, Russian troops will seize Ukrainian territory and take back Crimea as well as invade eastern parts of the country. For the moment, stillness possesses the nation. All is relatively quiet and stable.

The resulting collage of my sometimes-solitary life and travels during my tenure in Poland and Ukraine draws upon materials that roughly mimic Wordsworth's "spots of time," for this book assembles those passing, often seemingly insignificant, sounds and sights that remain in substantial lineaments and still invigorate the mind. Sad, absurd, aesthetically pleasing, ugly, painful, humorous, endearing, discordant, frustrating, reassuring, distressing, and often trivial, these spots of time do not fall prey, I trust, to the sterility of hollow generalizations. Rather, through their multitextured, multilayered, and overlapping particularity, these episodes remind one that a place is as intricate and as varied as the people and the landscape that structure its province. Never disowned by memory, these collected moments, like the long dry wind, still blow through my ears and beg to be recorded.

CHAPTER 1:

SEED TIME

There are in our existence spots of time,
Which with distinct preeminence retain
A renovating Virtue . . .
—Wordsworth, *The Prelude*

Before I commence the narrative of my experiences in Poland and Ukraine, I must first pause and return to the origins of my journey to these countries, to the seed time of my life. Most particularly, I need to revisit the day in 1946 when, as a child, I met Dr. Novak. It was this indelible moment that was to launch my curiosity about Central and Eastern Europe as well as to send me on my subsequent travels—hence the book's title, *The Odyssey and Dr. Novak*.

ENGLAND, 1946-53
This is where the odyssey begins. The time is a warm English summer afternoon in 1946. The place is the front garden of

the Unitarian parsonage situated in a modest town barely six miles north of Manchester. Holding my six-year-old hand is Dr. Novak, the head of the Unitarian movement in Czechoslovakia. He has come, perhaps (what does a child know?), to talk with my minister father about such matters as the postwar recovery in Prague. Four years earlier, the Nazis had murdered Dr. Novak's predecessor. Behind us, rhododendron bushes bloom; a garden wall half conceals a row of unkempt trees. Then there is nothing. The wreckage has been removed. No longer can one catch a glimpse of the seventeenth-century dissenting chapel peering through the oaks' limbs, for, during the night of December 21, 1940, German incendiary bombs destroyed this historic building.

While air raid sirens wailed in the dark, my parents, protecting a ten-month-old child and waiting for their own destruction, crouched in the cupboard under the stairs of the parsonage next door. On that same night, another incendiary bomb fell on the Victorian Sunday school building across the road, but because the device miraculously landed in an open toilet bowl, nothing happened. (Later, during the mid-1950s, when this building finally crumpled—a victim of a sinkhole—remembrances of wartime social gatherings, as well as the sounds of young nursery school children, descended, like Persephone, into the earth.) In the 1940s devastation was everywhere, for this community lay close to factories, mines, and textile mills. Ruins were a normal part of my childhood and played with my imagination.

When I glance at the snapshot, my attention, as if drawn by magnetic force (there is no way for me to resist), hastens to the compelling gaze of the figures in the garden. I see and remember a prim child all too willing to bury her hand within Dr. Novak's kindly grasp. Or did I reach for his? The two of us stand before the Kodak or the Brownie in a pose of affectionate understanding. He leans ever so slightly toward me. There's a kindred fondness, a bond that, for me, was to extend miles and years beyond the frame of the moment. I can still see his slicked back hair (it lies as full and as coarse as a badger's back); his eyebrows, which hang like a cliff's promontory over the depth of his eyes; his tailored suit (the buttons seem tight—is the suit a leftover from a younger time?); and, most of all, I remember his elegant walking stick as well as his erect figure and polished shoes. Dear Reader, do I sound too much like Jane Eyre? But I never saw or heard of him again. I do not even recall his first name. What happened before or after remains a mystery. Did he disappear into the maw of the Soviet machine that was to crush a yearning, among many Czechs, to maintain contacts with the West? Was he arrested and imprisoned?

In spite of all the changes to come, that summer day in 1946 resisted the tyranny of alteration and circumstance. Rather, salvaging itself from the rubble of time, that afternoon lingered long, defying the narrow days of life, and grew incorporate into me. In particular, the kindly pressure of Dr. Novak's hand imprinted itself indelibly on my youthful mind and later led me beyond the garden wall of my childhood to Czechoslovakia and then to the USSR, Poland, Ukraine, and Belarus.

Directly after World War II, other Czechs came to my father's parsonage. Their visits reinforced my attraction to Eastern Europe and contributed to curiosity's charm. There was Ludik Benes (also from Prague), a young man whom I adored and followed from room to room. I have no photograph of him, but I do possess a slender book, *Little Paul Dombey (Dombey & Son): A Charles Dickens Story Told for Children*, that he presented to me as a parting gift. On the title page he wrote: "To my little friend Anicka 15th Aug. 1946." Ludik was visiting because he was part of an international team of young Unitarians, the International Religious Fellowship (IRF), attempting to promote a better understanding among people of different nations. Fervently, yet delusively, idealistic, the group had rallied its forces and was meeting for a week in Manchester, during which period Ludik boarded at the parsonage. Two years later, when the Soviets seized full power in Czechoslovakia and were purging the so-called "dissidents" from all levels of society, Ludik, as well as the other Czech delegates, was denied a passport by the Czech authorities. As a protest, the IRF ceremoniously elected him president in absentia. After 1948, Ludik Benes disappeared.

There was also Mrs. Kessler, who, to escape persecution and death as a Czech Jew, had come, via an anguished passage, to live in our area. (For several moments when I was writing this, I suddenly forgot her name and sadly realized that I had no way to recall it, no one to help me find it.) She moved to a bungalow a few doors from where Mrs. Rowe, my "second mother," lived.

To my young eyes, Mrs. Kessler seemed old, but she was probably in her forties. And exactly how she made the passage from Czechoslovakia to where we were, I did not know. All I grasped was that she was displaced. Mrs. Rowe took Mrs. Kessler under her wing. The three of us occasionally drank tea and ate rationed slices of bread and butter together. (Fearing there might be shortages, the Labour government introduced bread rationing in July 1946. Butter had already been restricted since January 8, 1940—the day before I was born. Affected by the rationing, I now consume more butter on my bread than is good for me.)

I liked to listen to Mrs. Kessler talk—I was attracted to her unfamiliar pronunciation of common words. Mrs. Kessler was a gracious, cultured person who spoke of art and music; even at the age of seven, I found pleasure in that. Her house was quiet. There was no one else—no photographs, just furniture. That had not always been the case, but I did not fully understand just what she had lost.

In 1947, I spent hours with Mrs. Rowe in her kitchen. There we kept a sharp lookout for the postman, who might bring some missive from Czechoslovakia. Like a couple of eagles balanced on an overhanging branch and waiting for a fish to swim through the brook below, we eagerly watched for the postman's bicycle to appear, drift silently down the road, and stop before the gate of 33 Park Lane. Through the open kitchen window, Mrs. Rowe handed the postman letters she had written on behalf of people desperate to escape Soviet rule.

As a naive seven-year-old, infected by Mrs. Rowe's contagious earnestness, I joined in her endeavors by standing on top of the kitchen table, from which stage I delivered stern homilies to fictitious Stalinist officials. (The script belonged to my imagination.) At the top of my voice I ranted against communism, censorship, and regulation. After a moment or two, the seriousness collapsed and Mrs. Rowe cried with laughter. Reveling in this catharsis, I continued to rage with more passion than ever. My playfulness was strangely raw, for I knew enough to sense how political circumstances had ripped apart the lives of those I had met and those Mrs. Rowe attempted to help.

In that same year I was sent off from home to a boarding school in Highgate (London N6).

> "Good-bye, good-bye, to everything!
> To house and garden, field and lawn."
> —Robert Louis Stevenson

At school, I lived in a building adjoining another, badly damaged by a parachute mine. The ruins were strictly off limits, but we dared each other to scramble among the piles of rubble and hide among the weeds, which, like a phoenix rising from the ashes, had reclaimed their existence. When I made that move, my memories of Dr. Novak, Ludik Benes, and Mrs. Kessler diminished (but did not disappear), to be replaced, temporarily, by the reality of authoritative teachers who gave out conduct marks and enforced rules (the stale leftovers of a late Victorian era) that governed most minutes of the day -- though there were the Sunday walks in the Highgate Cemetery, where, in "crocodile" lines, we passed by Karl Marx's grave and saw where his followers left flowers. While my fellow boarders strode on, eager to get back to their afternoon tea, I turned my head and cast one more glance at Marx's larger-than-life dark-granite head. I knew enough to realize that even though Marx had been born in Germany and had lived in London, his writings had inspired the ideology of Eastern Europe. My early curiosity about that area of the world had not departed entirely.

During my time in boarding school, when Mrs. Rowe wrote to me, she said not one word about her campaigns to help those fleeing from Soviet oppression; rather, missing the child she had never had, she sent poems that in her Lancashire best she had once recited, at my insistence, over and over again. One was "That Tempting Apple Pie." Her round bright face, her crescent forehead framed by thinning short curls, and her pursed mouth had gleefully shaped each word:

> *One day, Mumsy Pig made a fine apple pie,*
> *And till ready to cook it she put it up high;*
> *But Piggy and Wiggy discovered it there,*
> *And to get it, they simply climbed up on a chair.*
> *Soon they cut it and greedily ate the wet paste,*
> *For they said 'twas a shame such a good pie should waste.*
> *But Mumsy Pig caught them and put them to bed,*
> *And for dinner they'd physic and water and bread.*

In a very loud voice, she had always added, "an natty mediton"—her version of a child's attempt to utter the phrase "and nasty medicine."

Late in 1952, my parents suddenly announced we were emigrating to America. We were to leave in February 1953. One result was that Mrs. Rowe came to visit us in London, to see us for one last time. During her stay, in the rainy autumn, on what seemed to me a sad, long, unlovely street (I did not want

to make the move), we met with two Czech refugees with whom Mrs. Rowe had corresponded. They had recently arrived in England. In their presence, remembrances of Dr. Novak, Ludik Benes, and Mrs. Kessler yet again haunted my youthful mind.

As poignant as this meeting in London was, one other morsel from this disruptive period of my life remained, refusing to be brushed into the litterbin of forgetfulness. Immediately before we were to be interviewed and approved for emigration by an official from the American embassy, my mother took me aside and tearfully begged that I not utter the word "communism." ("We will not be allowed to enter if you mention the term—and don't tell them about the people who live across the street and display a hammer-and-sickle banner in their window.") The specter of communism and Russia from my earlier childhood had, a few days before, drawn me to our neighbor's house. Curious as ever about anything to do with Eastern Europe, I had stood staring at their flag. Aware of the hysteria surrounding the McCarthy hearings investigating communist infiltration in the United States, my nervous mother feared I might say something that would cause us to be denied "alien" status.

PRAGUE 1969

In America, years passed, and I was married. My honeymoon was not conventional. In 1969, caught in the curious undertow of my childhood imagination, I spent the first weeks of my married life not only revisiting England but also crossing into a territory that had once been vividly in attendance, yet inaccessible, if not forbidden. After spending several weeks with Mrs. Rowe, my new husband and I traveled, via ship and train, to Prague and Bratislava. I was thrilled that I was actually going to be where Dr. Novak, Ludik Benes, and Mrs. Kessler had once resided. My fantasies were to become more tangible.

The summer of 1969 was a strange (and, for me, exciting) time to be in Prague, for it was just over a year since the so-called Prague Spring. Commencing in January 1968, broad-based governmental reforms had begun to soften rigid communist doctrines ruling the country. Under Alexander Dubcek's government, Czechs dreamed of democratic elections, greater freedom of speech and religion; they wished to abolish censorship, institute industrial and agricultural reforms, and end restrictions on travel. When we arrived in Prague, however, these hopes had been dashed or at best compromised. Exactly a year before, on August 20, 1968, two hundred thousand Warsaw Pact troops from the Soviet Union, the GDR, Bulgaria, Poland, and Hungary had invaded Prague in what was the largest deployment of military force in Europe since the end of World War II. Alarmed by what appeared to be the imminent collapse of communism in Czechoslovakia, the USSR ordered these troops and their tanks to roll through the streets of Prague. En masse, the city's residents gathered in the streets and protested against the incursion by blocking and climbing over the tanks, tearing down street signs to confuse the soldiers, identifying and following cars belonging to the secret police, setting up underground radio stations (journalists had tried to prevent the troops from taking control of Radio Prague), and sacrificing their lives. More than one hundred protestors were shot. And in January 1969, a student, Jan Palach, protesting the suppression of free speech, set himself on fire in Wenceslas Square.

When we arrived in Prague a few months later, in the summer of 1969, the sensation, if not the fact, of a hostile, invading Russian presence lingered on each street corner and hung around the doorways of buildings. Dubcek, the reformer, had become increasingly isolated and had been replaced by a "realist" willing to cooperate with the Soviets. Many of Czechoslovakia's intellectuals and business elite had fled, if they could, to the West. The people passing us in the streets were tense, confused, damaged, and distrustful.

I have memories of arriving in the train station and wandering with grudging assistance until we found a rather drab hotel with an available room. My college German was helping a little, but the street signs were still down so when we actually found a place to sleep, we were relieved. Economic difficulties were visible; there was not a sense of plenty, especially when we spent two days in Bratislava and wandered aimlessly around faded, damaged buildings that lined depressed streets like discarded rags. Shopping was difficult too. Goods I took for granted were neither plentiful nor available. I never found out how to buy sanitary napkins (what are now euphemistically called "feminine products"); therefore, I was a mess and uncomfortable much of the time (and annoyed with myself for not having anticipated my needs).

Finding a place to eat was always a challenge. Not recognizing the food and not knowing the language, we found a cafeteria in Prague where we pointed to the tray ahead of us and simply motioned "the same." I more often than not ended up with boiled tripe—a dish I despised but that was a favorite of my mother's—a taste developed during poorer times.

Unguided, and always a bit lost (sometimes giddily—we were young), we strolled alone through Prague's streets, gazed at the splendid architecture, and crossed the Charles Bridge (occasionally, whether I imagined it or not, I sensed we were being followed). Eventually George Zidlicky, the brother of one of the Czech refugees whom Mrs. Rowe had sponsored, took charge of us. The arrangement had been made ahead of time.

With the Zidlicky family, we took pleasure in the warm, relaxed, and lighthearted moments. Within their home, along with the men, we ate generous portions of meat and potatoes while the women sat behind our chairs, watched, and waited for us to finish; we visited George's butcher shop, where he vigorously wielded his sausages, and joined George's wife and her potato-peeling friends in the stone courtyard adjoining their house.

Only George spoke English, so we communicated with gestures and smiles—and perhaps with a few phrases of my halting German, a tongue uncomfortably familiar to them through

Nazi occupation. But there were also sobering, anxious episodes that resurrected thoughts about the circumstances surrounding the refugees and visitors from Czechoslovakia I had met during the immediate postwar period. In particular, I recall George's discomfort when he took us to the historical sites, such as the Prague Castle and Wenceslas Square—places where the militia was conspicuously in attendance. In less populated areas, fearing we were being overheard by an invisible secret police and frightened of their hawk-like surveillance (their "eyes so sharp that they can even see whose trouser-strap has come undone on the other side of the pavement" [Gogol]), George periodically whispered that we should keep our voices down. Casting furtive looks, he hastily led us away from spying ears. On the street, he was as wary as a stray cat. He refused to come near our hotel.

Walking the pavements where those I had known had once strolled was exhilarating but paradoxically upsetting, for, strangely, their absence became more definitive than before. So vivid in my childhood, they really were no more. The closer one draws to a memory, the more it dissipates. Being where they had once breathed left me with a better understanding of what had formerly troubled or disrupted their lives. I had a more immediate sense of what it must have been to be subjected to a hostile, authoritative rule. Though the visit reminded me of loss, it also opened doors.

USSR, MAY 1985

Years elapsed, and marriage ruptured. Eventually I met Irving Massey, a professor of comparative literature, whose fluency in Yiddish, Russian, and Polish nurtured my fascination and made it more possible to travel in Eastern Europe. In May 1985, both of us, curious to see with our own eyes the landscape of the Soviet state, spent two weeks on our own in the USSR. Intourist, the official tourist bureau, arranged our accommodations and transportation.

Among my first memories is the train ride from Helsinki to what was then Leningrad. When we boarded the train in Finland, we were put in a private compartment reserved for foreigners. From time to time, a stout, officious uniformed woman came in to check on us and serve tea. It was when the train stopped at the Soviet border that what had been a moderately comfortable ride turned sour. Thick-booted guards entered our compartment, pulled down the trap door in the ceiling, inspected it for contraband, and then demanded to see our papers and search our luggage. Irving is not the neatest of scholars, so pages and pages of notes and piles of index cards, among which was an address book, spilled out of his cases. Frustrated with his mess, the border guards demanded I leave the compartment. After several minutes, I grew worried and tried to force my way back in. (I had watched too many 1930s spy films; my imagination was creating a dire scenario.) No success, for a guard blocked the door and yet another pushed me up against the corridor window. I gave in and waited. Soon the guards left with Irving's address book in hand. I rejoined Irving, who was none the worse for the interrogation. We waited at least an hour. The book was finally returned. It had been photocopied.

We were on our way, moving through the Russian countryside, past rows of silver birches, and thinking of Gogol, Pushkin, and Tolstoy. The train started to slow down and—like an old dog that, on its afternoon, walk stubbornly sits down and refuses to move any farther—obstinately came to a full stop. After a few confusing minutes, a passenger poked his head around our compartment door and told us that the train had broken down. Complaining about the heat of the day, he encouraged us to exit through the carriage doors, breathe in the fresh air, and sit for a while on the grassy bank by the tracks. A leap and we were out among the wildflowers, the tall swishing grasses that stretched their fingers toward the cloudless sky, and the Russian passengers, lolling about, enjoying their release. The whole character of the journey had shifted. People were relaxed and singing; one man gallantly handed me a bunch of flowers he had plucked from an adjoining meadow, and even more surprising, the stout matron took off her tight wool uniform jacket, undid the top buttons of her blouse, and while displaying distinct cleavage, flirted and flitted like a pastoral nymph with a willing passenger or two.

A whistle blew. The Arcadian idyll was over. The train had been fixed. It was time to reembark. Another shift. People returned obediently to their cheerless seats; the matron buttoned up her blouse and resumed her bureaucratic posture. Such was the introduction to what, for the passengers on the train, was a normal schizophrenia—a state of mind oscillating between a darkening oppressive authority and the radiant sensuous sentimentality of a nineteenth-century Russian novel.

Once we were in the Leningrad station, an Intourist guide, immediately recognizing us, swept us away in a long black limousine, down the middle lane of wide thoroughfares normally reserved for officials until we reached our hotel, the Hotel Europeiska, where ladies at desks, placed by each lift and on every floor, watched our comings and goings, night and day. Our room was bugged so we spoke discreetly.

During the luminous days and white nights in Leningrad, on foot, we explored the nearby Nevsky Prospect, a grand boulevard designed in the eighteenth century by a French architect. A verse describing the Nevsky Prospect from Pushkin's "The Bronze Horseman" came to mind:

> *The empty thoroughfares, past number,*
> *Are piled, stand clear upon the night;*
> *The Admiralty spire is bright;*
> *Nor may the darkness mount, to smother*
> *The golden cloudland of the light,*
> *For soon one dawn succeeds another*
> *With barely half-an-hour of night.*

Instead of the packs of wolves that had once roamed this area, sculptured stone lions with one foot in the air guarded eighteenth-century buildings, vaunting their former splendor. Lining both sides of the concourse were palaces, theaters, opulent homes, financial institutions, cathedrals, monasteries, museums, naval headquarters, government offices, and once luxurious shops. At all times of day, streaming past these structures, masses of people flowed up and down the boulevard: pen-pushing civil servants, office workers, financiers, housewives, business men, children going to and from school, bureaucrats, shopkeepers, tradesmen, and, as Gogol once observed, people dashing off from work "to visit a friend from the office who lives on the third or second floor of a derelict building, in two small rooms with hall and kitchen" ("The Overcoat").

Occasionally, individuals extracted themselves from this torrent of pulsating humanity to pause and look through a shop window. If one wanted to get nearer to see the goods on display, one pushed the person blocking one's view—a behavior that alarmed me until I learned that there was nothing hostile in the gesture. And occasionally someone left the multitude to fill his mug with kvass, a drink made of fermented bread, from a tankard on the back of a wagon parked at a street corner. The striking contrast between the dense movement of the people on the broad pavement and the empty stillness of the road added to my sense of the schizophrenic culture we had entered.

Such incongruities were to accompany us in Moscow. When we arrived, we stepped off the train into a crowd of unfamiliar faces and waited for our Intourist guide. He was not to be seen. Instead, out of the swarming masses of tired, anxious passengers a petite, bow-legged elderly lady, as if an apparition disembarking from the past, quietly approached. Barely making herself heard above the sound of the hissing steam expelled from the train's massive engine, she asked Irving, in the most polite and elegant Volga Russian, where the toilet was.

The Intourist machinery had faltered; no one had come to meet us. We felt disoriented. Thanks to Irving's fluent Russian, however, we eventually found a taxi driver willing to take us to our hotel. On subsequent days, we were not left alone—someone was always visibly trailing or covertly listening to us. In the meantime, on the way to the hotel, while Irving chatted with the driver, I, unable to join in, tried to make sense of where I was. Gazing through the vehicle's window, I caught sight of enormous brilliantly colored banners, as long as ten stories high, hanging in multiple rows from Stalinist-style buildings. Displaying massive images of hammers and sickles as well as imposing portraits of political leaders, this drapery impersonated the clichés of my imagination and belonged to a fictitious set, designed for a grade B thriller.

In the days that were to pass, however, I came to realize that such theatrical scenery was more of a reality than not. These authoritative banners surveyed and regulated everything: the people waiting for hours in orderly queues to view Lenin's tomb, even the monotonous, repetitive run-down stalls selling the same fur hats in the once-grandiose Gum Department Store, a building that stretches a quarter of a kilometer along the Kremlin's walls. The ghost of Stalin and his lethal policies now cast a deathly pall over Gum's granite, marble, and limestone gothic arcades. (In 1928, Stalin converted the building into offices, and in 1932, when his wife died, he used the space to display her body.) This opulent structure had deteriorated under the weight of economic difficulties, repressive Soviet regulations, and State control. On the third tier and out of sight, however, a luxurious clothing store was still open but only to the highest echelons of the Communist Party.

Being Jewish, Irving wanted to visit the synagogue in Moscow. Not knowing the way and having only an address, we took a taxi. When we arrived and stepped onto the pavement, an elderly man, descending from nowhere, hastily warned us in

Yiddish, "Be careful—the rabbi is KGB." Like Hermes, god of the golden wand, once the message was delivered, he went on his way and soon was out of sight. Puzzled and slightly shaken, we entered the synagogue and spent a few guarded minutes with the rabbi who seemed superficially pleasant and interested in supporting the aging remnants of a Jewish community. But how to judge? Subject to scrutiny, he too led a double life and had to make compromises.

On another afternoon, we met with relatives of a Buffalo Russian friend. We had tea in their crowded two-room apartment, where four people lived. Shelves of books and objects, as well as boxes piled from floor to ceiling, took up most of the available space. After tea, we went for a walk. One of the men was extremely nervous. I recall turning a street corner and his urging us to walk quickly and keep quiet. The incident took me back to Prague in 1969.

Our departure from Moscow was fraught with difficulty; we almost missed our plane to New York. Annoying, rule-ridden, niggling customs officers took hours searching our luggage and would not let us through. We were trapped. In the nick of time, an official, who wanted us out of the way, interceded and rushed us to the departure gate. Breathless, we dashed up the rickety steps leading to the plane. The exiles must, for the moment, return home.

PART ONE

POLAND, 1995-96

What had commenced with Dr. Novak's visit to postwar England was fated to carry on, but this time for a more extended interval. Beginning in 1995, I was to reside and work in Poland for an entire year. What follows, I trust, captures the nuances of a life lived in the midst of political and social change. Dreams of economic advancement as well as fantasies of financial success were enticing the public and intermittently intruding upon their remembrance of the country's sad and vicious history.

CHAPTER 2:

TANGLED THREADS

WARSAW, SEPTEMBER 1995—JUNE 1996

*And I seek the land of the Poles that is lost, that is
not yet lost. Some say nearly lost, already lost, lost
once more . . . lost to whom, lost too soon, lost by
now, Poland's lost, all is lost, Poland is not yet lost.*
— Günter Grass. *The Tin Drum*

In September 1995, strands of communism as well as remnants
of Soviet rule are unraveling and clumsily intertwining with
the government's increasing commitment to a Westernized
economy. Old loyalties are at odds with entrepreneurial dreams
of growth and private wealth. Ambition, anxiety, and owner-
ship clash with collectives, unions, and a nostalgia for the security associated with a socialized state.

Poland does not float on an expertly crafted rug that magically rises above the complexities of what is below and ahead

so that its rider, in the twinkling of an eye, can be borne thither and land in a place difficult to reach. There is no flying carpet to help Poland find its way. Rather, this Central European country bumps along on a strangely woven fabric through which the warp of the East and the weft of the West incompatibly cross or pass over and under each other.

I am reminded of the time an American friend who, when visiting me in Warsaw, was attracted to a dazzling colored Indian skirt for sale, among other inexpensive clothing, on an outdoor market table reminiscent of an old Soviet style of commerce. She joined a group of women sifting through the garments (like ravens, they foraged by taking turns); selected a skirt; slipped it on over her clothes, and then crossed over to the window of a brand-new Western boutique in order to see, in its distorting, reflective surface, whether the item fit her or not. In the mirror image, a view of her cheaply produced skirt overlaid that of the tailored, luxurious clothes adorning the mannequins standing in the window. These contrasting images partially obscured and blended into each other to create an imperfect collage of a period in which one style of living visibly bleeds into and incompletely superimposed itself on the other. The two merged in the frame of the shop window to fashion a composite portrait of Poland's complexity.

Another swing of the hips to see if the skirt would do; the bystanders nodded their approval, and my friend, in spite of some doubts, purchased the item and joined the Poland of 1995.

Few escape such a baffling mélange of style and orientation. The sight of an elderly woman, shuffling every day to the post office, where she sits and compulsively reads a letter she either wrote or received years ago, is a weirdly disturbing anomaly in a culture that awkwardly and unpredictably mixes the present and the past. Nothing new overlays the news she reads. Clinging to and engaging the fading syntax of a former time, the woman sorrowfully bends over the missive's vanishing ink and mouths each precious lingering word in silence.

For most who pass by on the street outside, however, no single recurring document either defines their lives or keeps them aloft. Instead, the tangle of the then and the now keeps them alert and in suspense. As they go through their day, they never quite know which thread of ideology or circumstance will snag their progress. At times, an entrenched bureaucracy that stamps everything and won't look at anything unless it has an official seal on it governs, frustrates, and trips them. In the post offices, flush-cheeked women, sitting at desks piled with wobbling packages and heaps of mail, bang rubber stamps three or more times on every letter that comes through the slot. Stamped *POCTA POSKA* in violet, the letters start their journey or fill laundry baskets marked DEAD LETTERS.

At other moments, the craving for riches and the desire for the so-called comforts that a Westernized economy promises overtake and propel their lives. Taking advantage of this longing, pyramid businesses prosper. Herablife, an international company that sells a concoction (one is not allowed to call it medicine) that supposedly increases the quality of life, preys on women seeking a magic carpet into the middle classes. Booths, hurriedly erected on the streets of Warsaw, display pamphlets about Herbalife; people dash by sporting "I Love Herbalife" buttons, and cars— festooned with Herbalife logos—drive determinedly past icons of poverty. They speed past a ten-year-old beggar-gypsy boy who plays Vivaldi on his violin at the corner of ul. Nowy Swiat.

Not all followers are believers. Some just wear the company's badge so as to work the system cynically. Fully understanding the irony of her actions, Agnieszka, a bright and cunning feminist scholar, decides to take advantage of Herbalife and its exploitation of women's dreams. Needing extra money so she can fly to London and buy books on gender theory, she signs up to be a translator for an Herbalife convention to be held in Warsaw. After a week's work, she earns $3,000. Soon, with the money in her pocket, she disappears on a LOT flight to Heathrow.

For all these reasons, in 1995 my entrance into Poland is not easy. On several occasions, the tangled threads that complicate life in Warsaw ensnare me. In particular, the sharp, cold-edged remnants of an older Soviet bureaucracy initially snag the tissue of my wellbeing and compromise my commitment to new responsibilities and work.

The customs office in Warsaw is a setting for trauma, a knuckle-whacking introduction to a system where one must know which strings to pull, what bribes to offer, and what lies to tell if one is to endure.

The tale begins: Before leaving Buffalo to spend a year teaching at the University of Warsaw, Irving Massey and I, ship, via an agency specializing in mailing possessions to Poland, fifteen boxes packed full of books on American literature (I am told they are impossible to buy or to find in the libraries; I plan to give them to the Institute of English Studies Library), a small portable printer, clothes, shoes, cosmetics, medicines, Kleenex, toilet paper, and even a bathmat. I have been wrongly led to believe that such goods will be hard to find.

Initially, the fifteen boxes are sent to the wrong city (somewhere in eastern Poland), held up in customs, and after a week, forwarded to Warsaw where they are refused clearance. What to do? The liaison from the Fulbright organization, Dorota Rogowska, armed with affidavits of my legitimacy, offers to accompany us and help retrieve our possessions. After a circuitous journey, we reach a dilapidated wooden shed tucked into some godforsaken puddled, grimy train yard almost hidden from view below a concrete bridge. Inside the building, swarms of people, like blind mice, shuffle and scuffle about in a labyrinth of bare corridors and in front of closed wickets or locked doors. No phone is available. We are cut off.

On the first attempt to pick up my boxes, we are summarily dismissed. Dorota's presence and her affidavits have no effect. For the following four days, we try and try again. Arriving early in the mornings, we wait in line with hundreds of others for our turn to speak to some entity enclosed behind a small barred wicket cut into a concrete wall. The scene is out of Kafka. Each bar in the grating surrealistically crops the official's face so that only a sliced mouth with its metallic teeth peers through it. On the fifth day, after hours of queuing (this time we hope in front of the correct window), we are just one person away from being attended to, but some experienced broker, clutching a fat pile of loose papers, barges in. He leans into the open wicket. His broad leathered rear sticks out into our faces. I hate him. He does not budge. Hours pass while some lengthy official business laboriously takes place. Time to close; the wicket slams shut. Dorota cries; I want to go out in the train yard, scream, and hit something, somebody, anything.

On the sixth day, the executive director of the Fulbright Commission, Andrzej Dakowski, joins us. Tears of impotency glaze his eyes. Nothing happens except I learn that if I pay $1,000, customs will release the boxes. I refuse. Wishing I could rub Aladdin's lamp so that Baba Yaga might appear and transport me "beyond thrice-nine lands" to a destination far from this hell hole, I contact the American embassy. Whoever is in charge refuses to help. He says it is my personal problem. I am stuck.

Desperate, Irving dredges up the name of a Pole he once met at his university in Buffalo. Professor L. plays a prominent role in the Polish government. (It is rumored that he hoped to run for president.) We decide to try. After several inquiries, he is found; we talk on the phone and arrange to meet. Salvation (perhaps), for the politician cum professor is willing to contact the head of customs on our behalf. Before escorting us out of his office, though, he takes us aside (his experienced fingers tug firmly, yet gently, on our sleeves) and deftly coaches us on how to offer a bribe (a good bottle of brandy) and to whom.

Two days later, after distributing the brandy to certain officials, I have secured an arrangement that I can claim my boxes—that is, *if* Dorota translates each packaged item into Polish and *if* I sign an agreement stating that I shall take all my possessions back with me to Buffalo, including the books for the Institute Library. There is no alternative; I concede. After all is signed and sealed, we return, with cash. In the back of the Fulbright van, we cautiously make our way behind the customs shed, pay a hefty storage fee (the system will realize some profit, for my boxes have been sequestered for five weeks), and finally collect my possessions. After living off two sets of skimpy clothes, I can now change into cleaner and warmer attire.

But not all is over. A week later, the Fulbright office calls to say that our visas are incorrect (they are for only three months). We risk deportation. I also learn that the paper I signed to retrieve my goods from customs will only be legal for three months. It's back to labyrinthine lines and locked doors.

Even though we had paid and applied for a yearlong, multiple-entry visa before we came, we somehow were not granted one. The process and expense begin again. I must get another letter from the rector of the University of Warsaw to say that I am really working at and being paid by the university. Dorota from the Fulbright office loses days getting this document. I also have to produce more photographs, fill out forms, and show an official document to say where I reside in Warsaw. Eventually, after three visits to the visa office—fortunately, not as far away as the customs building—and after standing in line with other anxious clients awaiting their turn to enter through a solidly closed door, I receive my work visa from some entrenched, sardonic, sourjowled, middle-aged man who rules from behind a set of bushy eyebrows and a desk piled with papers and disappointment.

In the meantime, Irving has his own battle for a proper visa. He brings in evidence that he has already applied for a yearlong visa but is abruptly turned away because he does not have the same last name as I. The official, this time a matronly blond, does not believe we have come together so will not grant

Irving an extension unless, she adds, he is legally my husband—
and that (she regards us accusingly) we have to prove. We stand
as calmly and as patiently as we can before her experienced,
distrusting eye. In the end she says she would accept a certified
letter from the American embassy to say that we are married.

We are not. I must lie. Pumped up on adrenaline and
propelled by the forces of necessity, I seek out the American
cultural attaché, whom I have already met, and ask him to
compose a letter. I make up some cock-and-bull story about *not*
thinking I would need to bring our marriage license to Poland,
so it remains among documents at home. Furthermore, I fib,
there is not enough time to send for the license because the visa
office demands to have proof in two days. He must produce a
letter immediately or else. (Would he mind if I suggested some
phrasing? I ask.)

The kindly cultural attaché swallows the fiction, avoids
eye contact, and promises to have one ready. I should pick it
up in a day or so. (Will I be found out? He'll look at my papers
and see I am single.) As coolly as possible and armed with a box
of chocolates, I later return to the embassy. Within minutes, I
pass back through its guarded gates with a typed, signed, and
officially stamped letter stating that we are married. Prevarica-
tion is my bedfellow. Fearing the Polish official will have either
changed her mind or forgotten the arrangement, I rush back to
the visa office not only with letter in hand but also clutching the
required brandy.

Relief when the officer, after annoyingly perusing the document for far longer than it takes to read it, picks up her stamp,
poises it tantalizingly in the air, and both suddenly and forcefully
pounds a new visa to life. Following that last, violent motion, her
stern, officious eyes disappear into soft furrows plowed by an
unexpected cherubic (yet knowing) smile. We pleasantly chat,
collect our coats, and leave. As I scamper down the building's
marble steps, a nagging reminder of another time shadows

the triumph of my lie. I think of the people who lined up anxiously, repeatedly, and daily in a similar Warsaw building in an attempt to flee Nazi persecution. Isolated from help, subject to some barely visible authoritative presence sequestered behind officious wickets, they filled out forms, displayed reams of documentation, and probably offered bribes. Death, not deportation, was their alternative.

I arrived in September. But because of these difficulties, it is not until late November that I can actually, once and for all, feel settled and start to engage fully in what I have come to do.

From September 1995 to June 1996, as a senior Fulbright fellow at the University of Warsaw, I teach three graduate classes to exceedingly bright students and, once a week, lecture for forty-five minutes to two hundred undergraduates on the history of American literature. That lecture takes place late Monday afternoons. I enter what was, before the war, a splendid nineteenth-century building (now pockmarked with bullet holes and spoiled by a broken-up and decrepit interior). I climb four flights of marble stairs, enter a large, deep hall lit by the remains of what were once sparkling chandeliers, walk to the front, and mount wobbly steps so as to take my place on a raised wooden stage. The stage looks out, as from a crow's nest on an oceangoing vessel, over a large, distant sea of desks lined up in endless rows. I can hardly make out people's faces. No land in sight except out of the long windows where I am able to spy cars going by as well as the sculptured head of some luminary that stares back at me with its historic stone eyes.

The head of the department has not prepared me for this task. The two hundred students have no texts, but I at least have a microphone. I muddle through the first lecture and decide that for every subsequent class I shall design a handout for each person. (I live in fear that the few copy machines, usually available in rickety, start-up commercial businesses, will break down, close, or disappear.)

My other classes are in a building on the elegant ul. Nowy Swiat. Every day, I trudge up six winding flights of stairs to narrow, dull corridors that lead to small shabby classrooms; an unlit foul toilet (lacking paper); and a peeling, bare-walled office, which has one desk, six hard chairs, six professors, and a telephone that from time to time falls off the wall. We take turns sitting at the desk. To get coffee, I descend seven flights to a *klub* that sells borscht (what my colleagues disparagingly call "dishrag soup") and *kanapki*. The one bit of warmth in the building is the porter's cubicle. He hangs up our coats, puts our mail in pigeonholes, listens to opera on the radio, and sells cigarettes, fruit drinks, Kleenex, and candy. Most endearing of all, with pieces of delicate string, he hangs small, lost objects, like tiny notebooks and lipsticks, on his door so that the lost can be found.

The porter offers an affirming contrast with the divisive atmosphere of my department. My colleagues (all brilliant, well read, and sophisticated) hate, fear, envy, and yet admire each other. Agata does not utter one word either to the head or to Tomek; Agniezka and Barbara do not exchange even a nod. Ambitious, cautious Ewa dashes in and out uttering polite nothings, and Nancy floats blithely above it all in a cloud of poetry. Neurotic, they are on special diets, suffer from stomach ulcers, or are anorexic. For all these reasons, at the end of most days, my colleagues, as if diving under the familiar blankets of their beds in search of protection or oblivion, find relief in leaving the front doors of the institute. There is comfort in plunging into the darkness of the late afternoon and joining the warmth generated by the crowds moving briskly along ul. Nowy Swiat.

The Institute of English Studies would wreck if it were not for the head, a Marxist, who forcefully and stubbornly, if not sardonically, steers and holds the program on course from her well-fortified office hidden behind a thick cloud of smoke produced by the industry of her chain smoking. Emma is the successor of the Institute's founder, Margaret Schlauch, a medievalist and a leftist who fled the United States in the 1950s to escape the persecution of the McCarthy congressional hearings, devised to rid the country of all those with communist leanings. Not wanting to be subject to the question "Are you now, or have you ever been, a member of the Communist Party," she settled in Poland, where she had family connections and where, during the 1950s, her political ideology would not be associated with subversion or treason. As a member of the University of Warsaw faculty, Schlauch compiled the first anthologies of English literature, and in this way introduced as well as formalized the study of British and American literature into the university curriculum. I am here to add to an American studies component of this structure.

Guarded by her savvy personal secretary as well as by her thick Scots accent, the present chair, Emma, is impervious to criticism. One does not disobey or challenge the department head. I tried once and failed utterly. She has her minion in the form of another Scot who is clever, drinks like a fish, chooses his research libraries according to whether or not they are close to a fine restaurant, and at home in the Scottish highlands keeps a flock of eighty sheep (managed by his wife). He complains to me that his dog nips the sheep too hard. He also advises me on the best mutton for eating.

Friendships are spotty. People are busy, preoccupied. All is work. There are moments of connection but that is the best I can say. Only occasionally do I catch a glimpse of what lies below the surface of people's present lives. And when I do, I am sobered by what emerges. Late afternoon, I accidentally meet a colleague at a nearby café. Before the last bits of cappuccino foam have left the rim of her cup, she tells me about her guilt toward her father. During World War II, he was sent as a political prisoner to Majdanek (one of the largest concentration camps just outside of Lublin). He survived by running through an opening in the barbed wire. When her resourceful mother, a trained pilot who was living in Warsaw, learned of his escape, she managed (through pull and bribes) to get a plane, fly it solo through enemy lines, and reach him. But when he came home, my colleague, as a young child, rejected him. Aged by use and beyond recognition, her father was and continues to be a stranger to her.

We are all strangers to each other. There seems to be no place to meet people casually; there is no center, except perhaps for once a month, when lines of faculty and staff queue up to be paid (in cash). At a central administration building, I join those who—clutching their identity cards—stand, push, watch, read, and make jokes waiting for their *zloty* to be pushed by an aged, varicose hand through a window. Once the money is collected, though, the conviviality dissipates and people sprint off in separate directions, unknown to each other. If I were here by myself, I would resemble the forlorn English-language instructor from Glasgow who hangs around the empty lobby of where

I live. He does not know what to do with himself so repeatedly asks the person at the desk for the TV room key.

Even the library system is fractured. Anyone interested in researching an American author has to work among four or five libraries that are neither cataloged nor coordinated.

In addition to settling into my work, I must also become accustomed to my accommodations. We are to live at the Hotel Sokrates, a residence on ul. Smyczkowa, run by the University of Warsaw for international faculty. This apartment building belongs to the bleak gray concrete of a Stalinist era. It sits erect and boringly plain on a scruffy lot next to the last tram stop. Children play with sticks in a nearby, rusted playground.

Inside, the place is basic. My apartment has institutional furniture, a washing machine (which leaks), and a microwave

(which I succeed in blowing up—toxic yellow smoke fills up the place until I throw the appliance onto a narrow balcony and bang the window shut), but no pots, dishes, towels, knives, spoons, carpets, dishcloths, or reading lamps. Fortunately, there is an outdoor market in an empty, muddy adjoining field, so during our first days, we scout its rows of unfamiliar booths to search for these necessities. Occasionally, there is no water; the management puts up a notice to say there will be none. On these days, a large water truck pulls up outside the hotel and everyone hastens down to fill up containers with water that is actually clearer than the reddish-yellow liquid that regularly drips through our taps. At other times, there is an announcement to say the hot water will be off for half the day.

The lift usually works, except when a piece of metal between the second and third floors comes loose and trips the mechanism. The toilet cooperates, but the shower floods. And the wiring is unreliable. When I first plug in my computer, yellow flames and blue sparks crackle out of the wall. Black streaks on the plaster register the fact that the Delta computer I have brought with me is cooked, dead. Thanks to the god of fortune,

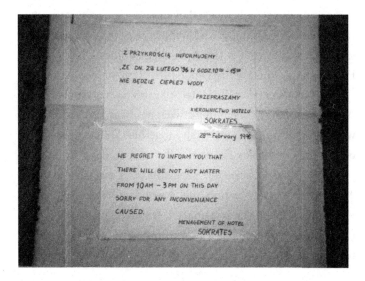

from the tram window, I spot the brand's newly erected corporate headquarters—a shiny, glass-windowed skyscraper that marks the coming of the West. Feeling like David standing before Goliath, I enter with my electrocuted computer and ask for help. Struck by my naiveté as well as my suggesting that it might still be under warranty, they look after me and arrange for the hard drive to be replaced without cost—unbelievable.

In spite of all these problems, however, the Hotel Sokrates is satisfactory, for it is secure and has a frugal bar (with stained tablecloths) that, when open, can be helpful if one has run out of food. The building is far from the cafés and restaurants found in the center. A brand-new, bright red-and-yellow McDonald's across the street is the only option. (I start collecting the toys that come with Happy Meals.)

If something goes wrong, members of the hotel staff fix it. Furthermore, if one needs assistance with the phone or directions, the hotel staff is there to help. Needing to get my hair cut and styled, I ask Anna, who speaks English and works behind the hotel desk, where I might go. Overhearing my request, a group of women lolling about in the lobby immediately gather around with suggestions while others, sitting in front of streaked picture windows partially blocked by tattered brown curtains, join in the game by sliding occasional pieces of wisdom across the lobby floor. They concur that I should go to John Louis David, a French chain, where stylists cut hair with razor blades.

What also makes the Hotel Sokrates more palatable is that Agata Preis-Smith, one of my colleagues lives here. Sometimes we go to and from the university together. Dressed sensibly in one of the two outfits she owns, she sprints along while complaining of headaches, liver problems, and a general malaise. The memory of her haunts me. I wonder if she is still alive. When I know her, she is damaged, frightened, and vindictive. Petite, skinny, taut, sharp-featured, and fair, Agata is incredibly brilliant and neurotic. Whenever we walk together, she insists on being on the outside so as to protect me from passersby and traffic. Agata exhibits a sense of decorum that I never fully understand. She is loath to let me see her flat because it is so messy. Indeed, as hard as I try, I never really comprehend her. At times she is silent; at others, uncomfortably confessional. With bitterness, she recalls the difficulties of managing during periods of want and, especially, of holding a young baby while standing for hours in lines with empty milk bottles ready to be filled; yet, when it comes to her turn, the official refuses and says the bottles are not the correct ones. Agata loses her place and must start again. She also speaks, with the rawness of an open sore, about giving birth (cesarean) without an anesthetic during the sparse communist years, when doctors told patients that pain is a sign of health.

Memories of that acute pain mingle with what she knows of her parents' past. Time has stripped their narrative, so what remains is a naked outline that is starving and will die. Agata tells me that as a young woman, her mother worked for the underground during the Warsaw Uprising publishing political leaflets and books. Subsequently arrested, jailed, and eventually put on a train to Auschwitz—not, I believe, the same trains that sent Jews to the camps—she seems to have led a doomed life. She survived, however, for she met a rich Polish baker who befriended her. Having lost his own daughter, he decided to adopt Agata's mother and pay for her release. (Polish political prisoners apparently sometimes had this option.) Saved by the baker, she got off the train at Kraków and found a safe haven with the family of her future husband, who, being an avid and young communist himself, had to escape in order to flee from the Germans.

In the Hotel Sokrates, Agata occupies a tightly packed, three-room apartment with her husband, Phil, a taciturn socialist who has lost his job (he emigrated from England to Poland fifteen years ago); their young son, who exhibits all the bright nervousness of his parents; and Agata's frail, aged, learned father, who sits, his threadbare jacket crumpled over a hand-knitted cardigan, in a corner of the cluttered kitchen. As much as his eyes permit, he reads. He is going blind. The rooms are chock-full of books. Her father rarely leaves the apartment. He suffers from heart trouble for which there is no help. They all live in fear of eviction, since Phil is no longer associated with the university.

The nightmare of Agata's life comes vividly back to me a few months later in the only letter she sends me after I leave Poland. It seems that one day her father left the apartment and walked out of the Hotel Sokrates to go and see an elderly friend who lived nearby. When Agata returned from the institute, Phil told her that her father had not returned. Agata assumed that he had lingered. When darkness fell and there was still no sign of him, they went out to try and find him. Agata paced back and forth on the pot-holed path that leads to the Hotel. He was not at the friend's place; he was nowhere in sight. On her way back, she saw what she thought was a drunk fallen over in the mud, averted her searching eyes, and walked by disgusted at an all-too-frequent sight. An anxious night followed.

The next morning the police showed up to say that a body had been found, dead, in the long grasses that waved in the cold winds in the rough empty lots outside the Hotel Sokrates. The "drunk" was Agata's father. Realizing that she had seen and walked past him, Agata struggled with the guilt of not having recognized her dying father. Full of self-loathing, she could not deal with the possibility that she might be responsible for his death. (I read her letter and realized she would tell no one at the institute about what had happened. Rather this incident, like so many, would join the strata of trauma and discontent that ran deep below the crust of her being.)

The tall, unkempt marsh grasses surrounding the Hotel Sokrates hide the dead and the living. I, too, have noticed the drunks who lie and linger with their bottles among their camouflaging stalks. Packs of stray dogs make beds out of the reeds bending in the breeze; their knotted shaggy hair flops carelessly over patches of mange. Squawking pheasants strut and scamper, avoiding the eyes of long-lost cats that dart and pounce through blades and lumps of weeds. When I come home late from the tram, I see that two dogs have treed a helpless kitten. With my umbrella extended, I foolishly, if not ludicrously, storm through the tall grasses and chase away the excited dogs. Later in the evening a fire engine roars up and puts out a blaze that has started in a nearby abandoned house, a shelter for vagrants. The children of Hotel Sokrates call it the Haunted House. The more the smoke rises and the more the firemen smash windows and search the area with weak beams, the more people open their windows and gaze into the troubled night.

The Hotel Sokrates is twenty minutes by tram number 36 from the center of Warsaw—that is, if all runs according to schedule and if there are no accidents or breakdowns along the route. On my way to get money at the American Express office, the tram suddenly stops. The driver beckons everyone to get off because the electricity on the next section of the tracks has failed. Everything is dark. After much discussion and grumbling, there is a rush to the nearest stop and consultation about what tram and when. On another day, the tram discontinues because a car has just plowed into a group waiting at the next stop. (These stops are narrow wedges in the middle of busy streets.) Seventeen are killed and injured. The police arrive and break up a crowd about to "lynch" the drunken driver. A week later, again I must get off. This time it is because someone, too eager to get to the other side of the avenue, dashes across the tracks; tram 36 hits and decapitates its victim.

To reach the tram from the Hotel Sokrates, one walks on broken concrete slabs past the wild lots and then waits and listens for the whistling of the wires that signal the tram's arrival. One learns that sound prefaces sight. Avoiding the begging gypsy women who park themselves daily at the stop, people cluster by the tracks and stare into the empty space of anticipation.

One morning, I join a taciturn group facing away from the wind. Our collective attention is caught by the lone figure of a middle-aged woman who, with her shaggy dog, approaches the tram stop across the tracks. Once she reaches the bench, she swiftly picks up her companion, places him on the bench, opens her wicker basket, takes out a brush, and in front of her unsolicited audience, commences her performance. She brushes her dog this way and that, turns him around and around, starts again, and then unceremoniously lifts his tail. While the dog squints, she vigorously scrapes through his whiskers and flattens his forehead with brisk and practiced gestures. When she finishes the grooming, back goes the brush into the wicker basket, down goes the fur into the closest rubbish bin, and off jumps the obedient dog. Satisfied that a morning ritual is complete, I and the other waiting passengers shift our attention and look down the tracks to see that the 36 is on its way. Whatever sense of community crystallized during the previous minutes dissolves when we hear the tram screeching as it rounds the curve and then listen to the sighing and groaning of its doors expelling passengers. Individually, we squeeze past each other up the steps and extend gloved fingers to stamp our tickets. On the tram, competing for space, I avoid the stale alcoholic breath of the rough-skinned man behind me, shield myself from coughs that curl around corners, keep my bag close, and worry unnecessarily about what news I might find in my mail box at the institute.

It is while waiting, exposed in the middle of the street for a tram, that one becomes acutely sensitive to the bitter cold of winter. The freezing air knows where all the gaps are in one's clothing. Like a cat that finds its way across the rooftops, it knows where the holes and the weaknesses are. It deftly works

its way inside and leaves shivering traces of its frozen fur on the skin. Even when one enters what seems at first to be a warm place, the cold follows. Either someone keeps opening the door so that drafts swirl around those seeking refuge within, or a person walks by and the air, like a stone thrown into still waters, responds by dancing in chilling rhythms about the back and down the neck. I have learned the technique of scarves. I wear a soft woolen one inside my coat, then, outside it wrap a long, wide scarf numerous times around my neck and over my mouth. I am not sure when I last did not wear long underwear. I refuse, however, to wear the popular fuzzy, half-mauled berets, sold in the street markets, or purchase the coarse fur caps, some in the shape of baseball caps that look as if the animal has just been pulled out of a trap and is now skulking around a person's ears. I buy, instead, an elegant Italian black felt hat.

For all my sensitivity to style, however, I am neither willing nor able to walk in high heels over sheets of ice. Rather, necessarily sacrificing aesthetics to survival, I daily pull on ungainly sensible ugly boots to navigate slippery streets. It seems there is no alternative. Imagine my amazement when, one frozen evening, on my way to a performance by the Polish Radio Symphony Orchestra, I notice fashionable, middle-aged Polish women, wrapped in sumptuous perfumed furs fringed with bouncing baubles and perched on high stiletto heels, pecking through the ice and speedily passing my shuffling steps. Clicking along and blithely unconcerned about falling, they link arms with their silk-scarfed husbands, wearing elegant winter coats worthy of a Warsaw tailor, and reach the concert hall ahead of me. How do they magically negotiate the ice as if it were a fashion runway? Left behind, I resemble some ill-shaped, flat-footed Kraken stirring from "his ancient, dreamless, uninvaded sleep" (Alfred Tennyson). Once inside, these women and men stand critically before large public mirrors and unself-consciously prune their plumage; they rearrange bits and pieces of their hair, makeup, and attire, as if sculpting statues of themselves. Elsewhere, they would study the windowpane's reflection to make sure their hats were on straight. How different from the quick, furtive looks we take at home in public spaces. What I do not realize at the time is that these people are not necessarily well to do but are subscribing to a culture that respects fashion and encourages a person, no matter what his or her means, to look stylish. They do not own many outfits (perhaps three), but what few dresses, coats, and suits hang in their bedrooms are cherished. The furs, exuding an insect-powder fragrance, are probably rented for the season or for a single afternoon.

In 1995, Poland is feeling the bite of an extended winter. People find their way in the crisp, dry, windless cold, behind flurries of large snowflakes, amid silent, thick snowfall, or beneath a frosty waxing moon. From time to time, Siberian winds gnaw on Warsaw, and leave the leftovers of their gorging on the ice. Warsaw looks bleak. Its gray concrete structures touch and smear the sky for months. My winter shoes are falling apart and my long underwear is full of runs and holes. Week after week on the tram I see no difference between the gray-whiteness of the sky and fields. Young people on their way to classes do not walk; they make slides out of the ice and glide along where I would fear to fall.

The snow is still blowing around me when I get off tram 36 this evening. As I walk away from the stop, the tram's overhead wires momentarily burst into electric blue and for a few seconds all of us move visibly toward our destinations. Inside the apartment, I look out of the narrow kitchen window into the frigid darkness and across to a single lit window on the second floor of the nearby army headquarters. (We blame this structure for the bad reception we get on BBC.) All the other apertures are as dark as night. Inside this suspended illuminated space, two officers play table tennis to pass the time. Their bright darting movements in the coldness of the late evening are mesmerizing and reassuring.

Low temperatures are stubborn, omnipresent, and perhaps even omniscient, for they know how to find one's most vulnerable and exposed areas. When I learn that more than one hundred people have frozen to death on the streets of Moscow, I believe it. God, it's cold. Today we hang a pair of Irving's just-laundered woolen socks on the balcony; in five minutes he comes to show me the icicles dangling like stalactites from their heels and toes. The other day I looked out of the window and exclaimed, "Shadows!" For the first time in weeks, the sun had come out for a moment and I could see the pattern of our balcony railings imprinted on the balcony's concrete floor. In Poland, shadow is a form of color. But winter is not relaxing its hold.

Outside the Hotel Sokrates, gray-beaked ravens strut about the frozen ground and grope among the dead leaves for whatever they can forage. It is a difficult winter for them too. Each morning, I bring them bread that we have not finished. I throw it over the barbed-wire fence surrounding the nearby military compound. Waiting up in the trees, they fly down, floating, swooping, and dropping like abandoned cloth handkerchiefs conversing with the currents in the air. Some mornings, I forget and guiltily walk by. On the ground, they sit in the snow. In pairs, they lean toward each other, as if supporting themselves and retaining what warmth remains under their ruffled wings. They seem to plead with me:

> *"Build me my tomb," the Raven said,*
> *"Within the dark yew-tree,*
> *So in the Autumn yewberries*
> *Sad lamps may burn for me.*
> *Summon the haunted beetle,*
> *From twilight bud and bloom,*
> *To drone a gloomy dirge for me*
> *At dusk above my tomb."*
> —Walter de la Mare, "The Raven's Tomb"

I also feed a pair of fancy pigeons living near the garbage container. Their feather socks quiver in the wind.

Escape from winter is required. The Eagle Club at the American embassy is pleasant. Occasionally on bleak days, I go there to eat American food, read the *Herald Tribune*, and watch marine guards flirting with daughters of diplomats. At other times, I push through the shining brass doors of the nineteenth-century Hotel Bristol (once the headquarters of the Nazi Party; Elizabeth Taylor also slept here) and take a seat in the classy Café Blikle. Under an autographed photograph of Arthur Rubenstein, I savor delicate pastries while looking across the room at a large mirror. Hung at an angle, it frames and reveals the slicked hair of the Warsaw wealthy, the blank faces of customers staring into their fantasies, the triangle of a silk handkerchief peeking forth from a gentleman's breast pocket, and the bowed faces of women confiding in one another. Alone, I eavesdrop and listen to a young woman talk about the breakup of her last affair with a depressed TV sportscaster. (The reporter took her to Florida for a weekend but never left the room. Spending all his time shopping by phone, he bought seventeen shirts. And that was the romance.) And once, desperate to leave the dull grayness of the morning behind, I wander in to the Belvedere Restaurant, which used to be the *orangerie* on the Lazienki Palace grounds. I sit at a table surrounded by attentive waiters and large tropical plants hanging menacingly over my food. Uninvited sparrows flutter in and out of their leaves. Warm, humid air clouds the greenhouse glass and frames, by contrast, a surrealistic picture of the frost and snow outside.

While I am eating, a man passes by and catches my eye as if to say, "Do you know me?" I realize I do. How could I mistake the face? It belongs to Jerzy Urban, and I have seen his portrait in the *New Yorker*. He is a Jew who survived the Holocaust by hiding with a Catholic family but is now anti-Catholic. He is the former spokesman for the Communist Party in Poland but has metamorphosed, like so many, into a new capitalist and millionaire. He is somehow the essence of Poland. This genius and opportunist, this irreverent, crude, and sued man appropriately edits Poland's most popular satirical newspaper *Nie*. I look over to where he sits with his entourage and ask the waiter if it is he. The waiter responds in a low, respectful voice, "Yes, that's Urban."

Often to relieve the winter bleakness, Irving and I meet in the large lobby of the once-splendid but still-comfortable Hotel Europeiski. Bits and pieces of the world pass through this lobby. One late afternoon, members of an opera company from Venice that has come to perform at the Wielki Theatre in Warsaw stand either huddled in a corner or melodramatically draped over the settees. They have just learned that their home, the historic opera house in Venice, has burned to the ground. Every last one (and there are about fifty) anxiously puffs a lit cigarette. The lobby fills with smoke. While I wait another afternoon, my eye turns to a pale young man carrying his violin and approaching a person who is to take him over to the symphony hall to perform a Brahms concerto. Even though they are running behind time, the violinist begs the person to wait a moment. The violinist disappears and returns with a large chocolate bar. It is not easy being a performer in winter. The oboist from Tafelmusk slips on the ice and breaks his arm; a pianist friend sprains her ankle and must practice for weeks with her leg elevated.

Sometimes the sun comes through and shines for an hour. On those days, rather than hiding in coffee shops, one finds one's way to Lazienki Park near the center, and joins others who have come out to catch what rays they can. Sipping a steaming cup of hot chocolate, topped with whipped cream, I stand close to the ducks in the snow and watch rows of people extending their open, seed-filled hands so that the black-capped chickadees can dart down, perch, and gorge on the offering. One Sunday afternoon in Lazienki Park, I approach a pond in which a mallard swims through ringed currents of melted ice. For a few seconds, the sun moves from behind a cloud and quite sud-

denly reveals the deep, brilliant oscillating green of the duck's neck. The vividness moves me to tears. It is the first color I have seen in months. A few paces on, I see the sun reappear and illuminate a peacock (introduced by the Polish nobility) perched on a classical garden statue. Its colors are exquisite. Juno would be pleased.

The Christmas season also offers some brief relief from the dullness. Warsaw is alive with Christmas lights and shoppers who shuffle over pavements of ice. Along the streets are booths where one can buy decorations. I go to a party at the ethnographic museum and buy some traditional decorations made out of straw. There, I meet a Chinese woman who is in Irving's Polish-language class. She tells me she has, just that very day, bought a factory.

By the beginning of April, the snow has almost gone. In its melting, I watch the rooks roll in the slush and take their first bath in months. Their obedience to the rhythms of their life is impeccable. Even when the cold weather persists, they dutifully build their nests, in clusters easy to see in the bare trees, and sit waiting for rebirth. Dirty patches of ice cling like a cracked, soiled epidermis encasing the earth's body; deep pools of water flood the rutted pores of the road. At street corners, choreographed groups of people jump back in unison to avoid being splattered by passing vehicles. As the thaw continues, from my apartment window I watch the occasional person walking his dog and become distracted by a car splashing in the puddles left over from last night's rain. A child's complaining voice echoes through the courtyard outside Hotel Sokrates and disrupts the reassuring sounds of the songbirds that have returned to the just-blossoming trees that grow behind the army compound.

Finally, the cold weather breaks, and all of a sudden it is hot. The gypsies who beg at our corner tram stop now appear in spotless white short-sleeved blouses. What people call "a Ukrainian summer"—a summer that bypasses spring—is upon us. All the windows on the tram are wide open. The cotton fluff from the poplar trees blows in and catches in one's nostrils. Every day for the last two weeks there have been thunderstorms in the late evening that have washed out the sky and left the air a bit fresher. Apple and chestnut blossoms have scattered.

On Easter Saturday, the blue sky brightens the pale green and yellow buildings in Old Town. People sit and face the sun. In Lazienki Park, among patches of snowdrops, it seems as if the whole of Warsaw is out enjoying the sunlight and queuing for *lody* (ice cream). While waiting over an hour for my cone, I watch children pick up stones and draw designs in the sand to pass the time; I give money to an elderly woman who does not have enough grosze to buy some popcorn. In the nearby amphitheater, I join many others who sit, heads tilted and eyes closed, to face the sun. Swans and ducks walk on the remaining glistening ice. A layer of water stands on top of the ice, which when it melts releases the trapped leaves of autumn.

The next day is equally welcoming. Irving and I decide to explore a nature reserve, a few kilometers south of us, that we have seen outlined on a map. We get on a bus and go too far.

The bus driver stops especially for us and gives directions about how to walk back, a hike that fortunately takes us by a little cake shop that is open and sells soft drinks. Once we enter the woods, we join hundreds of people who are just as willing as we to get out, feel the warm air, and tramp for hours through a maze of muddied paths.

May is the time of nightingales. I long to listen to their voices in the passing night and hear what Keats calls their "plaintive anthem."

> *Thou wast not born for death, immortal Bird!*
> *No hungry generations tread thee down;*
> *The voice I hear this passing night was heard*
> *In ancient days by emperor and clown.*
> *Perhaps the self-same song that found a path*
> *Through the sad heart of Ruth, when, sick for home,*
> *She stood in tears amid the alien corn;*
> *The same that oft-times hath*
> *Charm'd magic casements, opening on the foam*
> *Of perilous seas, in faery lands forlorn.*
> —John Keats, "Ode to a Nightingale"

In the evenings, poking my head out of the apartment window or stepping in pajamas onto the balcony to brave the cooler evening air, I catch the sounds of the nattering rooks and magpies and pretend that among them is a nightingale:

"That's one—do you hear it?—over there."

"Yes, maybe."

"Let's call Phil and ask if he has heard them yet."

Phil, my colleague Agata's husband, in the middle of the night last year, shouted out: "I wish those ruddy nightingales would shut up."

Phil is not in to help, but over the phone, I persuade Agata to warble like a nightingale so I might better recognize its call. She tries but says she has done it all wrong.

The quest seems impossible until along comes Barbara, an ornithologist, who for over thirty years has been mapping the bird life in a forest ten miles north of Warsaw. I met her through a friend. Barbara works for a low wage at the Academy of Sciences and lives in a rundown building. The lift smells of urine and her one-room apartment stinks of the two cats she rescued from her basement. She takes me in hand. In a few weeks, I am on my way with her to the woods. We start out at seven in the evening, just at the moment when the murmurous haunt of mosquitoes is at its fullest. Ingesting and inhaling them, we walk a few kilometers, through verdurous glooms and winding mossy ways, then put on boots and sludge through a swamp in the deep-delved earth, up to our knees. "Darkling I listen." My breath is quiet. I finally hear nightingales and the requiem of these "light-winged Dryads of the trees" ("Ode to a Nightingale"). But there are other sounds: rails resonate like pigs, and the calls of warblers, robins, and cuckoos fill the darkening air with a rippling music that fades away into the leaves, until their voices dissolve "into the forest dim."

Barbara shows me where a wild boar has been digging up the earth and where the badgers have been searching for grubs. She checks the nests (what she calls "her nests"). Stooping, she inspects the blackbirds huddled at the base of trees and then approaches a shrike's nest, where she lifts the mother off her fledglings to make sure the young birds are well. After all these years of her solitary daily visits, they let her near and allow her touch. Is it a vision or a waking dream? Unexpectedly, Barbara stops and whispers, "I hear a moose walking in the swamp." Slow, heavy, deliberate squishing noises draw near in the half-light of evening; the moose catches our scent and bounds out of the swamp and into the forest for cover. We too leave. Out of an "embalmed darkness," Barbara and I make our way to the road and reach home by eleven.

Not all is lyrical in spring. A friend visits during the Easter holiday weekend. The only restaurant open is at the five-star Victoria Hotel (the president of Poland works out in its health club). We have ten waiters to ourselves. Because it is late, we decide to take a taxi home. While waiting, we notice a group of well-heeled Poles, wrapped in furs, diamonds, and tailored cashmere, stepping out of their black Mercedes and swaggering into the lobby. Suddenly, distressing screams shred the fabric of their ostentatious wealth. Hearing their car door slam shut, they turn to see their Mercedes disappear into the night—stolen. The doorman, who was going to park their car (keys still in the ignition), momentarily stepped away from the Mercedes in order to obsequiously open the hotel door for these guests. In those seconds, an accomplice hiding in the bushes, jumped out, dashed into the car, and screeched away. By midnight, the vehicle will be across the Polish border and prepared for resale. Like a grouse protecting its family by feigning a broken wing, the doorman drops his extended arm so it droops at his side, simulates anguish, and pleads innocence.

In the mid-'90s, car theft is rampant. Two Fulbright friends, Denise and her husband Cliff, are robbed of the van they have shipped, at significant expense, from San Marco, Texas, to Kraków. Equipped with a lift and a special steering apparatus, this van gives Denise, who has multiple sclerosis, her mobility. One winter night after they return late from a concert, Cliff, exhausted from lifting and maneuvering his wife's wheelchair, decides not to park the van in the secure garage behind their building; instead, he leaves it on the street. The next morning, fighting disbelief, he searches desperately for some trace of the vehicle. Nothing, nothing is there. Calls to the police and posted messages are useless. Until a new van arrives from the States, their university in Kraków generously arranges for not only a car but also a driver.

CHAPTER 3:

THE LAND OF THE POLES THAT IS LOST, NOT YET LOST

KRAKÓW AND SURROUNDINGS

Warsaw and its immediate surroundings are not all I see of Poland. We make several trips to Kraków, a city saved from destruction by the fact that, in September 1939, it became the capital of the General Government under the colonial administration of Nazi Germany. During that period, many monuments celebrating the Polish national culture were looted and destroyed. Because the area's splendid medieval and Renaissance structures survive, essentially unscathed, Kraków is now an international tourist destination. Visitors meander through its standing historical buildings and wander around one of the largest medieval squares in Europe (the Rynek Główny).

This destination, with its cloth halls (originally designed for the medieval rag trade) converted into restaurants, shops, and entertainment spaces, functions as the center of tourism in the city's old town.

In the mid-1990s, people are also traveling to Kraków to amble through the remains of its Jewish ghetto, search among its tangled, overgrown cemeteries for familiar names, and stroll around Plac Nowy, the Jewish quarter's main square. When I am here, I see the beginnings of development that in the next several decades will bring cafés, museums, Jewish-music festivals, bookshops, hotels, and luxury apartments to the area. In the '90s, the legal disputes over these properties are complex, fraught with fear that the former Jewish inhabitants or their descendants will return to reclaim this real estate. Later, visiting Lodz with a Polish-Jewish relative from Montreal, we pass two middle-aged men, who, casting a disapproving eye in our direction, mutter to each other, "The Jews are back." Before World War II, Jews made up one-third of that city's population. By the time the war was over, the Lodz area had lost 300,000 Jews as well as 120,000 other Poles.

Although the old city of Kraków circulates around its grand central medieval square, I sense that its metropolis is without a core. My response, though, would upset those who adamantly believe that the city, once the capital of Poland, is still central to the country's well-being. Shaped by the length and breadth of its still-visible history, as well as by its aristocratic roots and long-standing contacts with foreign powers, Kraków, in their eyes, is not only still the capital of Poland but also eminently superior to a newer, fragmented, and scarred Warsaw. Like the bells of an ancient cathedral regularly marking the time of day, my critics would sound out the enduring rivalry between the two cities. Their preference for Kraków would reverberate and swell throughout the land.

In my mind, however, a nagging disturbing uncertainty, ambiguity, and divisiveness compromise the seemingly solid, enduring stones of Kraków's historical castles and towers; deep fissures run through the city's psyche. In the mid-1990s Kraków, it seems to me, gathers into itself so many contradictions that there is no place in which to rest my mind or securely settle my feet. Within its boundaries, invasions, massacres, beauty, grace, intellectual curiosity, greed, generosity, prejudice, bigotry, revolution, daring, conventionality, enlightenment, liberation, tolerance, and oppression either trip over each other or commingle in concentrated clusters to create a confusing, unbalanced setting. The city uncannily deviates from itself. I am uncomfortable, for instance, when Kraków celebrates the Jewish heritage it once silenced. It is strange being in a culture that listens to Radio Maryja (the voice of anti-Semitism and bigotry) yet simultaneously promotes Holocaust tourism. A devoutly Catholic provost at Kraków's prestigious Jagellonian University, founded in 1364, devotes his spare time to studying and reading Yiddish. What does one do with his desire or with a growing impulse on the part of the intellectual classes to study a language that they were once officially taught to despise and silence?

An express train runs between Warsaw and Kraków. In January 1996 after I have turned in final grades, we decide to go. The ride there is lovely with soft, comfortable red seats, a free lunch, and heat. The countryside looks beautiful. A tacit sun lights up the snow glistening on the long, sloping thatched roofs of the older houses and barns, shines on clusters of snow-covered birches and firs, and comes to rest on half-frozen brooks meandering through the fields. The train station in Kraków, though, has never seen the sun; dampness seeps through our skin there. The Saski Hotel, where we are to stay, near the main large square, is splendid from the outside. The lobby, featuring an old wrought iron lift with mahogany doors, is promising too. But the rooms are not. Basic and bare, with hardworking radiators that cannot compete with the tall, leaking windows, they offer cold comfort. A wool cap in bed is the ticket.

While Irving goes off with one of several librarians, all named Maria, to the French Studies Institute, the National Archives Library, and the University Library, I set out in negative twenty-five degrees Celsius through the streets to find the Ethnographic Museum. After dipping into shops en route to prevent my body from freezing, I reach the museum and find myself alone among exhibits displaying various costumes, masks (many racist and anti-Semitic), and folk sculptures worn or displayed during regional religious ceremonies. A dutiful guard follows me around. She turns on the light as I reach each room and switches it off when I leave. While I rather self-consciously and ignorantly (I cannot read the labels) peer at the exhibits, the guard sits in a folded chair and holds her head in her hands. What, I wonder, are her circumstances?

Not unhappy to leave this marginally awkward setting and longing for warmth, I go in search of a refuge not only from

the cold but also from my surroundings' puzzling paradoxes. Near the vast central medieval square, I reach the entrance of the Jama Michalika Café, established in 1895. Inside, the graceful art nouveau furnishings recall a softer time. The flowing stylized patterns of the café's tables, chairs, cabinets, light fixtures, and mirrors temper my recollection of the abrasive, forbidding double-walled fortresses as well as the commanding tower of St. Mary's (Bazylika Mariacka) just beyond the café's doors. According to legend, from the top of St. Mary's tower a trumpeter sounded the alarm before the Tatars invaded the city in the thirteenth century. Supposedly, an enemy's arrow pierced the trumpeter's throat mid warning. As if still alerting those within hearing, a trumpeter now plays at noon every day. To replicate the past, he always cuts short his call.

Secluded from this architecture of conflict, the café's Tiffany-like glass ceilings, windows, and intimate lamps exude warmth and comfort. While sipping hot tea and seated in a mahogany booth, close to a fireplace adjoining a turn-of-the twentieth-century cabinet, I gaze into oversize mirrors sus-

pended, at an angle, high on the opposite wall. Their blem-
ished surfaces gather reflected images of murals and paintings donated by students of the nearby Academy of Fine Art,
established in 1818, in exchange for free meals. On other walls,
discarded marionettes dangle on fraying strings. Starting in
1905, these puppets were used in cabaret shows protesting
bigotry and government censorship. Many satirically depict
once-prominent Krakówians.

In January 1996, cafés are welcoming spaces and Kraków
has many. In the Ariel Café in the old Jewish section, we devour
latkes while listening to old recordings of popular 1920s music.
This place feeds off Holocaust tourism: a Ukrainian group plays
Yiddish songs; waiters dress up as Orthodox Jews, sell Jewish
kitsch, and accommodate groups of young Israeli tourists who,
led in protective gatherings, troop through the ghetto as if conversing with the forbidden.

On another late afternoon, we go to a wine cellar, where
a draft follows us down the staircase; then one of the Marias,
whose family has lived in Kraków since the eighteenth century,
takes us to a charming coffee shop—the kind one expects in old
Vienna, with mirrors, plush seats, intimate booths, small round
tables, decorated walls, and chandeliers. Elderly, diminished
men and women lean over their espressos and cream cakes while
talking about who is there or just sitting and gazing at nothing.
When we leave, Irving kisses Maria's hand; she glows and a halo
of melted snow circles her feet. We return to Warsaw the next
morning. This time, the train is crowded and without heat. We
share the compartment with a family suffering from bad colds.

We are to return to Kraków several times in order to explore
its surroundings.

As many feel obliged to do, we travel sixty kilometers south,
by bus, so as to visit Auschwitz and Birkenau. I am uncomfortable with myself; I should not be here.

In the thinly scattered snow of late February, we trudge

through the shades of death and past spectacles of suffering into the gas chambers, the crematoria, the cells for political prisoners, the hospital barracks (where the medical experiments were conducted), the holding barracks, the women's barracks (where women slept twelve to a small bunk), the gypsy quarters, the latrine house, the warehouses where the prisoners' possessions were stored after being sorted, the mass graves, the long platform that leads into Birkenau, the commandant's house, and the officers' swimming pool. All are unforgetting witnesses to a pain that is never done.

This catalog of horrors prefaces another concentration camp, Majdanek, the second largest death camp in Europe, just outside of Lublin, that we later visit. The absence of hundreds of tourists plodding its empty fields—no foot marks their presence—as well as the nonattendance of the all-too-sincere yet transparently practiced dialogue of the Auschwitz guides, allows Majdanek the space in which to make room for the past. In the ensuing silence, death and remembrance reverberate. Alone and undirected, I wander into its still-intact gas chambers and feel what before I saw with "how blank an eye" (Coleridge's "Dejection an Ode").

Later in February, a Sunday midday meal in Warsaw occasions another vivid view of this unutterable past. Friends from Buffalo have come to see us and want to meet a middle-aged cousin of a Jewish American acquaintance. (Even though they have been warned that the cousin is "a bit odd," our friends are kind and concerned. They have come with money and a thick woolen cardigan for her.) During World War II, Rose was incarcerated in the Warsaw ghetto but miraculously managed to escape and flee to Russia. After the war, she returned to Poland, where she remains. Brilliantly fluent in many languages, she can facilely move from one foreign language to another. Rose now ekes out a living as a translator.

We all meet for lunch at a modest hotel located in a less-than-picturesque section of Warsaw, close to Rose's rooms. The hotel's restaurant is a dreary smudge of brown except for its crisp white linen tablecloths, which offer some relief to the eye. When Rose enters, removes her coat, and stands before me with her slacks unzipped, I know that not all is right. And when she speaks, I hear her chaos. Rose does not want anyone listening to what we say, so throughout the afternoon, she vigorously shushes our friends and instructs all of us to keep our voices down. Shadows of persecution and loss stalk her distorted life. Like so many Jews in Poland, she fears revealing her Jewish identity.

However, when it is time to eat, I more fully sense the damage of her earlier deprivation and maltreatment. At first, claiming she has an upset stomach, she refuses to order food. But as soon as ours arrives, she helps herself to the food on each of our plates, relishes it, and claims that she came in before we arrived to talk to the cook about fixing a special meal for us. By the time we finish, like a starving vulture suffering from a broken wing, she has devoured at least one-half of what we ordered. Then, retrieving a plastic McDonald's goblet from her carrier, she snatches tea bags from our china cups, one by one (her movements are as quick as a frog's tongue catching a fly) and repeatedly (at least ten times) asks the indulgent waiter for hot water. Nine bulging tea bags crowd a single container. To complete the occasion, she dips into her carrier and pulls out jars, which she fills with the salads we have not eaten. These leftovers go back in her bag. Then, after cleaning each plate as if a stern matron or guard were going to inspect it, she clumsily removes the platters to another table and with the side of her worn hand, compulsively, meticulously scrapes morsels of food off the tablecloth. There remains no evidence of anyone's having eaten anything. All is clear. She is safe for the moment. Before we depart, she refuses the money our friends have offered— in fact, throws it back—and exclaims that the cardigan is the wrong color. She does not want it. Her Polish pride refuses the gift. Our friends vow to try to see her again.

Buses from Karków also go to Zakopane, in the Tatra Mountains. In early March, we leave Warsaw in the rain and arrive in a fresh, thick, pristine snow that buries the mountains and swirls in the valley. The morning sky breaks so we join a line of skiers and take a lift to the top of Mt. Kosielec where we can barely see our way so must grope among half-formed images of those who have come for the sport. A few yards from a cluster of practiced skiers, I watch a lone, confused Englishwoman who, without gloves or hat or goggles, is being led by some sort of guide to the head of a trail. Her skis go in all directions at once. Does she survive? I never find out.

After a few minutes the clouds roll through the mountains and eradicate the perspective, so we descend to the snow-covered trails below. Water trickles through openings in the frozen streams. I stop to look at a European robin hopping among the waterweeds and pausing behind a yellow marsh flower. The daubs of red upon the bird's chest vibrate among the tints of

blossoms edged by snow. Farther on in the brook's rushing water, a dipper, a bird the size of a thrush with large strong feet and a most visible white throat, plunges into the current and walks on the stream's bed, occasionally, with its claws, lifting pebbles to catch insects. The clouds of morning move; we hire a horse and sleigh. Bumping along over places that are beginning to melt, we shield ourselves from the wind and tuck the sheep rug more tightly across our knees. The smell of the horse envelops us; the sound of the sleigh bells beat out our progress. All is tranquil, a pastoral, a picture postcard, until the horse sees the barn and breaks into a gallop. The driver's shouts and sharp tugging motions are impotent. We clutch our seats for dear life until the horse reaches the barn door, halts abruptly,

and reaches for his hay. Shaking, we gladly get off and return to the security of shank's mare.

From the train window on our way back to Warsaw, in the late afternoon, I glance at the melting corrugated fields; only the indented furrows are white. Just before evening, flocks of returning storks feed in the open areas next to gatherings of trees. Even in the darkling light, I recognize the redness of their beaks. Irving starts a conversation in Polish with our solitary companion, a man reading a book about the House of Potocki, one of the wealthiest and most powerful aristocratic Polish families that originated in Kraków. The Potockis have multiple estates and have been known through the centuries for their military prowess and cultural achievements – not to mention their vodka. Irving asks about the reading, a question that leads to introductions. The man is Jan Potocki himself, a direct descendant, a prince (and also a physicist). We fall silent, and he returns to reading his family's history.

The Tatras are alluring, so we return in early June to hike into a mountain lake. The path up is long, steep and still covered in ice. Once we arrive, we stare into the deep green lake and skate with our eyes, over its thin, translucent veil of ice. On our return, we meet a group of twenty-five chattering school-children with their teacher on their way up. She instructs them to step aside so we can pass more easily; they do and decorously monitor our slow, clumsy progress on this sheer descent. Once we have maneuvered past them, the teacher instructs them to bow and applaud. (Respect for elders is part of their education.) We are charmed and embarrassed. Soon a fox crosses our path and restores balance. Minutes later we hear the children's distant, excited voices spilling over into the lowering clouds. They have reached the lake.

It is difficult to leave such beautiful scenery and softness behind, especially when it is time to board the train at Kraków to return to Warsaw and its academic responsibilities. The train pulls into the station. Feeling chilled, I decide to get on as soon as the arriving passengers have disembarked. Everyone seems to have gotten off, so wearing my backpack, I climb up the steps and start down the train corridor. Suddenly a group of men, who seem to be in a panic, run out of a compartment and try to push by me. I think, *Oh, they have fallen asleep and think they have missed their stop.* In their rush to get by me in the corridor, they press me up against the wall. Eventually untangling themselves they get off the train and disappear. Confused, I open a compartment door and reach my seat. Irving suggests that they were trying to rob me. I insist that if they were, they did not take anything—that is, until I take off my backpack and find the zipper completely agape, my belongings all shuffled. When I discover that my wallet is missing and my identity gone, Irving dashes off the train to find a policeman. I worry that the train is going to leave without him. The Poles sitting stoic across from me at first ignore my distress, but then, quite suddenly, one of them—a middle-aged woman—rises, leaves the compartment, and, mysteriously, after a few minutes, without one word returns with my wallet, which, she gestures, was tossed onto the platform. Just the money is missing.

Lacking the words, I mumble sounds of gratitude. Like Madame Defarge from Dickens's *A Tale of Two Cities*, she returns to her knitting. Later when I leave the train in Warsaw, I distrust anyone who brushes by me. Two weeks after that, Irving is robbed while boarding a tram—an all-too-common occurrence.

Other surroundings of Kraków also attract visitors. In April 1996, when the rain turns the snow into deep slush, we board a local bus and drive from Kraków through the fog to visit the historical salt mines (a UNESCO World Heritage Site) in Wieliczka. After descending hundreds of twisting steps, we walk over four and a half kilometers in various levels of the mine, pass through long tunnels and corridors, and enter large rooms with sculptures, chandeliers, and chapels carved out of salt and luminescent crystals. Deeper down, we walk around a museum showing tools, machinery for lowering horses into the mine, treadmills, and clothing of the miners. The mine extends for many miles and is still active. Indeed, children and adults suffering from asthma often go there for the summer. The mines become a sanatorium. The air relieves their symptoms.

A swift and pitch-dark ride in a narrow lift brings us to the top again. The first time I took this restricting lift was a few months earlier when I was with a Fulbright colleague who suffers from claustrophobia. I suggested we sing our way up—I think the strange choice was "Onward Christian Soldiers." It worked.

GDANSK

Throughout the year, in addition to traveling to Kraków and its surroundings, we venture elsewhere. In the dead of winter (why, I shall never know), we take a train to Gdansk, on Poland's Baltic coast. (Before the Second Word War the city was a free state.) The seaside in winter beckons me. The snow falls, the winds blow, the ice forms, and we persist. Walking from the train station to our hotel on silent, nearly deserted streets, we occasionally shelter from the wind in the recesses of doorways.

We peer into the windows of the amber jewelry shops lining Marjanska Street (amber comes from the Baltic Sea). Few are open at this time of year, but those that are offer what they call a "winter discount." One jeweler gives me a special price because I am the "first" customer of the day. It is five in the afternoon.

Gdansk (formerly Danzig), a major seagoing and trading port for centuries, has many levels of history (most recently, the beginning of the Second World War and the birth of the Solidarity labor movement in 1980). Before the war treasures, patrician mansions, and handsome buildings displayed a catalog of the city's rich and privileged past, purchased from Teutonic knights and Polish kings. During the war, however, these structures tumbled and crashed into the elegiac, scrap heap of memory. In 1945, Gdansk's old town (with the exception of one fourteenth-century church) was completely leveled, just as was Warsaw's. The restored old section of the city now stands as a tribute to the compulsion to rebuild what was destroyed, to realize the legend of the phoenix rising from the ashes.

After the war, what did not survive was reconstructed piece by piece, detail by detail, ornament by ornament. Consulting prewar photographs of the area, the Russians painstakingly rebuilt and, in a sense, revived what had been bombed or burned—if only it were possible to reconstruct lives by transforming snapshots of the departed into living bodies that move and breathe once more. The result is a disturbing beauty, for what one sees is a facade, a front, a mere copy of former splendor. No matter how one tries to pretend otherwise, the past will always be ruined and silenced. A nagging sense that what lies before the eye is not real skulks on the periphery of one's vision.

The old town borders the city harbor through which large ships pass. Solid and still, these oceangoing vessels stand frozen and waiting. The ice packs in layers upon itself and seems even to freeze the facades of the area's tall, fourteenth-century Hanseatic League dwellings. The wind howls through the old city gates. In an open spot below a footbridge over an inlet, coots, mallards, and swans collect and wait for people to bring them crumbs. The coots stretch their rounded webbed feet, the mallards stand or crouch, and the swans tread clumsily on the ice. Only when they fly and extend their long, graceful necks do they regain their dignity. When they pass directly overhead, I hear their wings rhythmically swishing up and down and listen to the subdued sounds gurgling deep in their throats. Long gone and far from fantasy are the prewar summer days that Günter Grass remembers in *The Tin Drum* when:

Chimes sent pigeons up in clouds: to cry. But all about was laughter. Women with sunburned children, terrycloth bathrobes, brightly colored beach balls and toy sailboats, descended from trams bearing freshly bathed multitudes from the sea side resorts of Glettkau and Heubude. Drowsy girls licked raspberry ice cream with lithe tongues.

After the war, people wear a different look. Men seem demobilized and women smiled while concealing an undertone of the sorrows they've suffered.

Not far from Gdansk is Europe's largest castle, originally erected by the powerful Order of the Teutonic Knights in the thirteenth century. From Gdansk it is an hour's train ride to Malbork Castle. Once inhabited not only by the Teutonic Knights and later by Polish royalty but also, in the 1930s, by the Hitler Youth and the Nazi League of German Girls, this castle was more than half destroyed at the conclusion of the Second World War. A 1945 photograph shows the devastation: shell-damaged walls gaping and pockmarked, arrested avalanches of stones spilt from bombed towers, and brittle charred roofs hanging precariously over piles of rubble. It was not until 1962 that restoration of this site began. We come when that work is well on its way. Now only the main cathedral is still in ruins.

We arrive on Saturday afternoon, just one hour before the castle closes. We are the only ones there. It is freezing cold. Irving finds a guide who is willing to take us around. She speaks Polish but puts in the occasional German word (sometimes a Russian phrase interrupts her thought). She takes us

through one magnificent room after another. The vaulting, frescoes, fireplaces, windows, tapestries, and thirteenth-century doorways (still showing their original paint) are wonderful to behold.

The guide is loquacious. Irving pretends to follow her patter and does to some extent. She seems pleased to have our company. Taking hold of my hand, she proposes that we walk outside the castle by the River Nogat. People are ice fishing; dogs chase swans, and children slide, with and without sleds, down slick shining hills sloping from the castle to the water. The guide starts to tell Irving about herself. With her ungloved hand she writes in the snow the date of her husband's death; he was run over by a bus in 1974. The lovingly written numbers will dissolve; unlike the refurbished castle, nothing can restore his life.

To get back to the road, we scramble up an icy hill. Incredulous children show us the way. We return to the train station and eat a snack; then Irving searches for the "toalety" but does not know how much to pay for its use. He approaches three skinny young girls clustered like sparrows behind a counter (the only people in the deserted station). As soon as they see him, they start to giggle and chirp. He asks them "How much?" They turn away and consult. Eventually one comes back and, wryly cocking her head, inquires, "*Pissoir* or *cabinet?*"

Blushing, Irving replies "*Pissoir.*" That will be thirty groszy.

We go out to the platform. Drunk, black leather-jacketed teenagers lean daringly out of an open train window and jeer menacingly at a group of Polish army men walking just in front of us. The army men wait until the boys are at a safe distance and then coolly raise a finger. Our train arrives and takes us back by Malbork Castle now glowing red in the evening light as if a fiery wreck—a memory of its earlier destruction. We share a compartment with a man on his way to Warsaw to take advanced classes in taxation. Once a farmer (his parents are now alone on the farm), he closes his accounting textbook so he can go to the window and show us the landscape's rich soil in which "everything grows well." He too has not lost a memory. Like so many others rushing to join Poland's rising middle classes, he is studying to become an accountant and is exchanging the countryside for the city. But he still feels the soil beneath his fingernails and treasures that earth.

THE PLACES OF EARLY SUMMER

In hot late May, we go northwest from Warsaw to Torun. On the five-and-a-half-hour bus ride, people strain to open unwilling windows to let the stifling air circulate and blow through the stuffy interior. Turning toward the window to catch some breath, I notice storks sitting on their nests; their beaks extend beyond the dense elevated mass of branches.

In Torun, we buy gingerbreads made in ancient molds in the shape of horse-drawn carriages. They are solid; one risks breaking a tooth. Before it is to be declared a UNESCO World Heritage Site in 1997, we walk in the yet-to-be-developed old town where Copernicus was born, stroll downhill through ancient gateways, and reach the river, where hushed barges slowly move their cargo upstream. Farther on, we come to a small zoo where a black bear circles his shadow in an iron cage and where dingo dogs, in a small enclosure, howl and jump, all four feet in the air, whenever the keeper walks by. These images play in the mind like motes in the eye.

In the weeks remaining before we leave Poland, we take a bus to the village of Kazimierz Dolny, 147 kilometers southeast of Warsaw on the right bank of the Vistula River. There we buy bread in the shape of roosters and crayfish, wander in the old town square, walk among the castle ruins, visit an old Franciscan monastery, and go past a synagogue turned into a movie house. Surrounding the village are walking paths that meander through orchards bordered by blackcurrant bushes. All is sweetened by the early-summer light.

In the woods, we visit the remains of a Jewish cemetery (1850–1930). Like sentries guarding history, each gravestone stands at a distance from its neighbor among the trees. The Nazis once used these *matzevot* (gravestones) to pave the streets of the town. Long shadows of reflected branches lie across these stones, pied and mottled by the sunlight peering through the leaves. Their wraithlike limbs connect one spent life to another.

The following weekend we travel three and a half hours by train to Poznan—west of Warsaw, not far from the German border—and accidentally attend the finals of an international violin making competition held every five years. A young man from Italy wins. He is one of 180 entries. Before receiving a free glass of wine and bacon-flavored potato chips, we listen to two sonatas played on the winning violin. Afterward, the evening

is still young so we walk up the hill to a Franciscan church and attend a chamber choir concert.

The next morning, a few kilometers from town, we enter a park dedicated to beekeeping. Hundreds of hives from the fourteenth century on, each more decorative and imaginative than the next, fill the park, as do children dressed as bees, drawing pictures of bees, and dancing a "bee dance."

On our return to Poznan, we walk by the synagogue, which the Nazis transformed into a swimming pool, and which still stands as such, and come to the old town square, where we find a café, sit, eat, and watch people go by. At the next table are two loud German tourists who have come to Poznan for the weekend. Their presence reminds us that, although the borders between Poland and Germany have often swung back and forth, Poznan is now really a satellite of Germany, which, I believe, finances much of the town's infrastructure and businesses. People are more abrupt and businesslike than those in Warsaw; this city has a harsher edge to it. Yet all is forgiven when I stroll down one of its narrow streets, pass an open window, and overhear a bass voice practicing an aria and a violinist rehearsing a passage from a Scarlatti sonata.

Later, we spend a day in Lodz. I recall little except the streets bordered by deserted textile and cotton mills, six or eight stories high. In the mid-nineteenth century this city was the main textile production center of the Russian empire. The thudding din of the steam-propelled looms pounding inside the factories would have reverberated through openings in the brick walls and joined the clatter of weavers' clogs in the exterior courtyards to create a cacophony of hard work and hard times. Now doors and windows are boarded up, smashed, and scrawled over with graffiti. The mills' whistles that once called people to their shifts no longer blow. All is hollow and silent. Only weeds flourish and push their way through chinks in crumbling bricks. Not a soul is to be seen.

I walk through this wasteland and remind myself that striking workmen once staged protests outside these walls, the largest of which took place in 1892, and that in 1905 Tsarist police viciously fired upon and killed groups of Polish workers carrying placards denouncing the autocracy of the Russian empire. The area reminds me of the Manchester—the industrial North—of my childhood; I cannot help but be drawn subjectively to its landscape. I am back.

*It was a town of red brick, or of brick that would
have been red if the smoke and ashes had allowed
it; but, as matters stood it was a town of unnatural
red and black like the painted face of a savage. It
was a town of machinery and tall chimneys, out
of which interminable serpents of smoke trailed
themselves for ever, and never got uncoiled. It had
a black canal in it, and a river that ran purple with
ill-smelling dye, and vast piles of building full of
windows where there was rattling and a trembling
all day long, and where the piston of the steam-
engine worked monotonously up and down, like
the head of an elephant in a state of melancholy
madness. It contained several large streets all very
like on another, and many small streets still more
like on another, inhabited by people equally like
one another, went in and out at the same hours,
with the same sound upon the same pavements, to
do the same work, and to whom every day was the
same as yesterday and tomorrow, and every year the
counterpart of the last and the next.*
—Charles Dickens, *Hard Times.*

CHAPTER 4:

INTO THE COLD

LVIV 1995

During the University of Warsaw's winter break, Irving and I cross the Polish border in order to reach the most westerly region of Ukraine and then travel fifty kilometers to the city of Lviv, now one of Ukraine's main cultural centers. Irving has come to continue his work on philo-Semitism and Leopold von Sacher-Masoch's Jewish stories. Lviv has the bulk of the author's papers.

Before the outbreak of the Second World War, the city was a vital core of Polish and Jewish culture. Its opulent libraries, palaces, royal residences, early municipal buildings, churches, scientific laboratories, castles, markets, the Ivan Franko University (founded in 1661), the neo-Renaissance-style Lviv Opera House (built in 1901), and even remnants of the so-called Scottish Café (to be renovated in 2014)—where, in the 1930s, a group of mathematicians collaboratively worked out research problems on the café's white marble table tops—attest to the city's rich cultural history as well as to the intelligentsia that once populated its institutions and overflowed into its streets.

Sadly, under both the Soviets and the Nazis, many of the city's intellectuals had been tortured, murdered, deported, or have since passed or moved away. The Soviet repression in the late 1930s, which sent many of Lviv's cultural leaders to their death in forced-labor camps, as well as the Nazi massacre of twenty-five university professors in June 1941, echoes in the memory.

For the next two weeks, we must find our way through a mélange of vociferous Ukrainian nationalists, less audible Russian sympathizers, devoted followers of the former Austro-Hungarian empire, scraps of Jewish culture, diehard German nationalists, and remnants of a once-dominant Polish presence. Subject to the wrath of history, Lviv has multiple identities. The city's variety of names says it all: Lviv (Ukrainian), Lemberg (German and Austro-Hungarian), Lwów (Polish), L'vov (Russian), and Lemberg (Yiddish)—and what is its designation among Armenians, who constitute one of the city's minorities?

As with so many other Eastern European centers, these various allegiances reflect a long (Lviv was founded in 1256), complicated, and often divisive and bloody past that is almost too intricate to map. Shifting borders, battles for control over the city, disputed territorial claims, invasions, dual authorities, multiple languages, mixed allegiances, armed uprisings, genocide, censorship, and deportation have continuously disrupted any possibility of an integrated sense of place and loyalty. The city's unparalleled architectural beauty (from medieval to art deco) is a memorial to this dappled past (the Germans did not bomb Lviv) and leaves the beholder wondering to whom does the city physically or emotionally belong: Austria, Galicia, Germany, Hungary, Lithuania, the Ottoman Empire, Poland, Russia, the Swedes, the Tatars, or Ukraine? All of these nations have, at some time, laid claim to it.

Only in the last few years has Lviv's primary allegiance been to Ukraine. In the period of liberalization from the Soviet system in the 1980s, the city was the center of political movements advocating Ukrainian independence from the USSR. After the dissolution of the Soviet Union in 1991, Lviv got what it wanted and became a part of independent Ukraine. In the 1990s, during its conflicts with Russia, the city harbors some of the most extreme Ukrainian nationalists, such as the members of Svoboda, a political party that bans atheists and promotes a nationhood built on "blood and spirit." It too is frightening.

What I saw and experienced in the frozen residue of 1995 would not be recognizable to people visiting present-day Lviv, nicknamed the "little Paris of Ukraine," where tourists might comfortably enjoy the architectural vestiges of grander times while relaxing in brightly ornamented coffee shops or strolling down manicured boulevards. Money has flowed in since 2012, when Lviv became a UNESCO World Heritage Site and the city turned its attention to attracting foreign visitors.

When I arrive in December 1995, tourism is not yet a priority; survival, however, is. Lviv is struggling to pull away from its Soviet past and is economically not at all well. Wrung out from its troubled history of shifting borders, languages, and allegiances, Lviv, like a dirty, wet rag, sits limply waiting to be resurrected and repossess its former glory.

In the mid-1990s, to those in Warsaw who have never been to these parts, Lviv represents an estranged and threatening world. Ukraine and Poland have often been at war over the possession of it, a city from which the Soviets expelled 100,000 to 140,000 Poles following the Second World War. Though occasional tentative connections, student exchanges, and even familial ties occur between Warsaw and Lviv, Lviv is generally regarded with fear and remains isolated. For most it is an unfamiliar destination, known only through horror stories about thugs in hotel lobbies and roaming Mafiosi. My friends in Warsaw are amazed we are going. They think it dangerous and advise me to hang on to my jewelry, not speak English too loudly, keep a low profile, and avoid crowds. On the train, be sure to lock your couchette doors. One colleague, however, speaks of the city's beauty and suggests that it combines the aesthetic pleasures of Vienna, Paris, Prague, and Kraków.

THE JOURNEY
The December 1995 journey to Lviv is a trip into the unknown and, as such, still rattles down the tracks of my memory.

With our passports close to our bodies and our money distributed in various pockets (we have to take American dollars), we arrive at the Warsaw-Gdansk Railroad Station at eight in the morning. The snow is blowing; the train station, lit by hollow, harsh fluorescent bulbs, is virtually empty, except for a few people milling around under rafters covered with puffed-up pigeons huddled and sheltering from the cold. Heeding the warnings of Agata, we speak softly, *sotto voce*. We are to leave from Platform 3, so, after crossing the tracks on foot, we join others either lugging massive plastic bags of goods or waiting silently.

The train looms out of the early darkness. Bulky, black-green, and full of smoke, it emerges from a Soviet past. We find our wagon and step into a dark, cold, and grimy world that will be ours not only on the train for the coming fourteen hours but also for the next fortnight in Lviv. A ghastly dimness makes it hard to grope our way through the train, feel our way past minute buckets of coal, and enter our second-class compartment. Mud, melted snow, and months of memory streak the windows. Ratty stained curtains, stamped in one corner with an official seal, slouch in a corner of the window frame. Bunks with blankets, knotted and inhabited by the germs of humanity's history, occupy both sides of the couchette. The pillows leak feathers; the covers are gray, rough, and used. A small table extends from under the window.

We are relieved to have the compartment to ourselves, for

the travel agent has told us that women and men are segregated on the train and that we, therefore, shall not be able to be together, unless we pay off the conductor. It is ours for an hour, until a university student, who is going home for the semester break, unexpectedly joins us. (Young people from Lviv quite often attend Polish universities.) Communicating with bits and pieces of Polish and Russian, we learn that she was ill after the Chernobyl accident. "I'm fine now," she claims. Once the polite exchange is over, our companion nimbly climbs up to the top bunk and disappears, dead to the world, under the bedding we have rejected.

When the train laboriously moves away from the station, we cannot conceive why it will take fourteen hours to go approximately 180 miles to reach our destination. Before too long, however, we begin to comprehend why the journey is to be long and dreadful. The compartment grows colder and colder. Soon we learn that there is no food or drink, so for the next fourteen hours we live off two small boxes of juice and three chocolate wafers we find buried in our pockets. The occupants in the adjoining compartment know better and have brought tins of sausages and bottles of sauerkraut. The putrid smell of our neighbors' repast coasts through the vents and mingles with the smoke from a coal fire the lady conductor stokes and on which she warms water for her tea. The toilets are too awful to use. A dirty rag lies over the seat, which is never cleaned. We both refrain.

From time to time the train pulls into stations and stops, but no one, it seems, gets either off or on. When we arrive in Lublin (the largest Polish city east of the Vistula River), there is perhaps a change of engines, and then the train seems to go back the way we came. It is now impossible to see anything out of the window. Though it is growing darker and darker both inside and out, there are no plans to turn on any lights. My feet are like stone.

After enduring seven hours of sitting in complete darkness, we come to an abrupt stop. Irving, with the help of a flashlight, has been snatching furtive glances at paragraphs from his novel while I have been listening to books on tape. When the Polish border guards embark, a few fluorescent lights magically switch on. The officials inspect our passports and then instruct us to leave the cabin so they can search for contraband. The lights go off and we are underway for a while, until yet another set of Polish guards enter and look once more at our passports; they carefully compare photographs to faces. Lights off and move. Soon the train stops again; lights on, and we are asked to fill out declaration forms that are written in Ukrainian (and in small print). What to do? The student in our compartment, like a groundhog from its hole, crawls out from the blankets and helps us while repeatedly exclaiming in Russian, "The trip is a nightmare!"

Lights extinguished; we proceed but not for very long. This time, the Ukrainian guards, wearing their heavy square fur hats, enter and take away our passports and tickets. In the freezing air, their breath trails their commands. After at least half an hour, they return with our documents. The train jerks slowly forward and finally halts at a station full of enormous machinery and lifts. It is like entering some leftover Soviet-style factory or perhaps finding oneself in a frame from a German expressionist film showing massive cogs and wheels laboriously turning, grinding, and producing.

As a relic of territorial disputes, the train is forced to stop because the tracks in Ukraine are not the same width as they are in Poland. They are narrow-gauge tracks, so in order for the journey to continue, the train's wheels must be taken off and narrower ones put on. (This anomaly was recently corrected; new tracks have been built, and high-speed trains now regularly whiz between Warsaw and Lviv.) For several hours, while still seated on the train, we are shaken, jolted, lifted, and pushed. Groans and clanks accompany the train's moving back and forth. I can stand it no more. I whip out my Sony Walkman and listen to a tape of Helen Reddy singing "I Am Woman"—anything to give me strength to endure the ordeal.

Finally, the train pulls into Lviv. Dazed from the long day that has been night, and not yet fully awoken from the nightmare, we step out into a dim station jam-packed with travelers on their way to I know not where. It is 11:00 p.m. Like lost sheep, we follow passengers down stairs and through unlit, filthy, frozen, dripping tunnels, through puzzling corridors, until we emerge into a domed nineteenth-century grand hall, adorned with clumsy imposing friezes displaying communist hammers and sickles.

Brimming with goodwill, our guide, Ihor Markow, greets us and leads us out into the cold night. Across the street a car, stinking of preserved sausages, awaits so it may bump us along to the Hotel Dnister, a place where foreigners often stay. Though our room is dull and modest, the hotel seems bright and clean. Famished and dehydrated, we set out on foot through deserted streets in search of a restaurant. The two places Ihor thinks might be open are shut, so we try the Grand (Mafia) Hotel—the one with armed guards and cell phones. The bar is open; we are thankful when the attendant agrees to make us sandwiches.

On the way back, a silent snow possesses the earth. Gentle circles of light radiate from the occasional wrought-iron lamppost and illuminate drifting particles of snow. The sight

softens my ragged fatigue. It was Lviv that, in 1853, introduced Europe's first street lights.

Unattended, the next morning we walk down to the old celestial city through a sloping park. Children sled and ski, dogs bound through the snow, and parents rush to keep up. Following our eyes (no map is available), we amble from one old square to another, past structures from the sixteenth, seventeenth, eighteenth, and nineteenth centuries. The streets below are thick with poverty, sorrow, sickness, and affliction. Lviv is in pain.

The trams are crammed because only a few can still run. Because the city lacks the means to build new ones, the older models suffer from inadequate repairs. In some parts of Lviv, water flows only during short periods of the day; the shops lack stock. Inside the historic buildings, one discovers neglect. The city cannot afford lights. We enter the ethnographic museum where nothing is illuminated and where exhibits sleep too long in the dark. At a gift stall we want to buy something but cannot properly see what is for sale. We ask the attendant to turn on a light; she shrugs, "It does not work."

LEOPOLD VON SACHER-MASOCH (1836-95): A PILGRIMAGE

In the days that follow, I initially accompany Irving on his quest to visit institutes and archives holding the papers of Leopold von Sacher-Masoch, who was born and lived in the city. Interested in the concept of philo-Semitism in nineteenth-century Lemberg, Irving wants to find out more about the composition and circumstances of Sacher-Masoch's Jewish stories as well as to examine the claim—or if you prefer, "legend"—that the writer is himself Jewish. The search leads to few definitive answers but reminds one that in Europe there is no such thing as being part Jewish. Any hint of Jewish ancestry and that is enough to label a person as such.

Fascinated with the various ethnic cultures that populated the capital of Galicia, Sacher-Masoch, spent much of his life writing stories, in German, about the region's Polish, German, and Galician inhabitants, later translated into Ukrainian, Polish, Russian, and French. In particular, in 1878 and 1881, Sacher-Masoch published two sets of Jewish stories in which he displayed a remarkably thorough knowledge of Jewish customs as well as affection for the Talmudic enterprise. (Irving discovers, however, that many details in these tales are plagiarized from other sources.) Nevertheless, these narratives intrigue Irving, as do Sacher-Masoch's various campaigns to work against local anti-Semitism through adult education and by means of a Leipzig-based monthly progressive literary magazine (1881-85) in which, as editor, he promoted tolerance and integration of Jews in Saxony.

These stories, however, are not what most people think of when they hear the name Sacher-Masoch. Rather, their attention leaps almost exclusively to his *Venus in Furs* and its exploration of sexual gratification through physical and emotional abuse. (Indeed until recently this was the only Sacher-Masoch book to be translated into English.) The book endures. Indeed, in one of those bizarre twists of history, a group of entrepreneurs in Lviv have now appropriated it to attract visitors and create a lucrative branding opportunity that, in their view, places the city on the map. Playing upon the popularity of *Venus in Furs*, these businessmen are promoting masochistic tourism. (And this is progress. The weird distortions of capitalism are depressing.) As a marketing gimmick, one Lviv businessman opened the Masoch Café, decorated with whips, chains, and bras, in which customers, both male and female, can choose to be tied to a chair and, among other painful delights, be lashed, by a waitress, across their bare backs. Outside the café stands a life-size bronze statue of the writer. All this is surreal, far, far removed from the Lviv of 1995, which revered his work and respected his interest in Galician culture. No intelligence can fathom it.

The eventual pilgrimage to find out more about Sach-er-Masoch's writings and life is fraught and difficult. It has as much uncertainty and complexity as do the questions concerning his Jewish origins. Strangely (because it is a Christian text) and perhaps inappropriately, all I can think of during this quest is a passage from John Bunyan's *Pilgrim's Progress*, for often *Ignorance* is our companion through this once-splendid city of Lviv, Lemberg, and Lvov. (Literary parallels sometimes assuage anxiety.) Bunyan aptly captures our dilemma as we try to find our way through the mysteries of ancestry and nationality:

> *So they went on, and* Ignorance *followed. They went then till they came at a place where they saw a way put itself into their way, and seemed withal to lie as straight as the way which they should go: and here they knew not which of the two to take, for both seemed straight before them; therefore here they stood still to consider.*
> —John Bunyan, *Pilgrim's Progress*

As the quest continues, *Vain Hope* joins us. The first stop is an attempt to locate materials in the Austrian Institute, yet another magnificent building gone to seed. After climbing wobbly, creaking backstairs and scuttling past unclean toilets, we enter a splendid receiving hall that proffers a view of the park and the radio towers that Russia erected to interfere with Voice of America broadcasts. (Nobody has bothered to remove them.) Alone sits a smart secretary typing at a desk standing on a fraying Oriental rug that partially disguises a cracked parquet floor that once shone and reflected the brilliance of the Austro-Hungarian Empire. In German, she directs us to an office where a diligent, round-spectacled Austrian suggests that Irving would do better to go across town to the Austrian library. (The Austrians are nostalgic for their historic presence here and maintain what they can of their former presence.) Off we go, back through the old town and ascend a hill. Having reached the Austrian library, we clamber up what was once a splendid flight of stairs, walk through an unmarked door, and enter the library's reading room. Disappointment: the archivist whom Irving needs is away on holiday.

Lunch is the only thought, so we return to one of the restaurants that was closed last night. It is Christmas Day in the West, after all. I feel the need for some sort of celebratory "dinner." (I should explain that in the religious calendar of Ukrainian and Russian Orthodoxy, Christmas comes several weeks later.) We enter a dim, cavernous room. The only glow comes from a tinseled Christmas tree attached to which is an electronic gadget that repetitively cranks out familiar seasonal music and traditional carols. A badly dressed doorman, waiters in crumpled tuxes, and a menu we don't understand greet us. We are one of two groups of customers. The restaurant offers little warmth. I take off my shoes and place my feet in Irving's sheepskin gloves; we wrap scarves around us. When the food arrives, it consists of blackened french fries (leftovers cooked innumerable times) and tough, dry meat. Freezing and disappointed, we eat and return to the center of Lviv so we might hunt for the Lviv Archives. At least Irving will know where they are located for another day.

After slipping and sliding across the darkening streets of late afternoon, we inquire at some sort of tailor's shop where we might find the door to the archives. An old, wrinkled, arthritic finger that has threaded many a needle wafts vaguely toward an imposing thirteenth-century wooden door that has bolts and locks the size of one's arm.

With a hefty push, it creaks open and deposits us in a stone hallway. We worry that the door will slam shut and we'll be trapped. Nobody in sight, so we knock on an inner door marked ST. ANN's. It's the wrong one. "Upstairs," we are told.

After winding our way up delicate wooden steps, we arrive at
another old entrance. We pass through it, open a more modern
contrivance that unexpectedly swings, and find ourselves facing
a lengthy, dark corridor that resembles illustrations representing the "vanishing point" in art. Seventeenth-century porcelain
stoves and framed medieval portals line each side of the hallway.
Which one should we go through?

Thankfully, a door opens and emits some promise of light
and heat. We enter. This time it is not Russian, Polish, or German that works for Irving, but French. Pleased to show off her
impeccable French, the librarian says that Irving should return
tomorrow and she will have materials for him. In my literary
frame, she appears as one of the virgins from *Pilgrim's Progress*
who will show the pilgrim the rare ancient documents. I enjoy
the walk back to our hotel through the park's quiet darkness.
That night we eat in the hotel restaurant, another empty room
with little heat and rumpled waiters. The food is not reassuring.

As they often do, mornings bring promise. For the moment,
Hope is our guide. We arise and go down to the chilled hotel
restaurant (where a tomcat shrieks), eat smoked chicken and
sawdust bread (with the additional delight of rancid butter), and

sip on apple juice. Irving takes a taxi back to the archives, which we located the previous afternoon. He has negotiated with the hotel staff for a ride; he has been warned that it is dangerous to catch a cab on the road because he could be robbed. Even though it is bitterly, biting cold, I decide to walk to the archives through the lovely park and take one more look at the historic buildings along the way. When I arrive, I find Irving conversing with yet another librarian, this time in German. She sits in front of an enlarged photograph of herself in army uniform. She is helpful and gives Irving more contacts and phone numbers.

Wearing my coat in the reading room, I sidle up as close as I dare to a porcelain stove that produces some semblance of warmth. Once in a while, another reader periodically leaves his seat to poke the stove to tease out more heat from its reluctant and aged orifice. In the poor light, while hunched over a Melville novel I am supposed to teach on my return, turning the pages with gloved hands, I occasionally glance at the rows of seated scholars poring over old maps and newspapers that in this semidarkness are barely visible to the human eye.

Irving keeps getting called away because people, once they learn of his interest, want to meet him. There is an alarmingly avid Ukrainian nationalist, who speaks English, and then a young German, who is researching German settlements in Ukraine. This young man insists on becoming our guide and wants to show us a cheap way to eat lunch. Like *Vain-Confidence*, he gallops ahead as we struggle to keep up and briskly falls into a deep pit. Much to our horror, he suddenly slips and slides on his back down the icy stairs leading to an underground passage. Concerned, we observe his recovery and marvel at his ability to carry on as if nothing has happened. We cautiously follow him to an outside stall, where he buys some sort of prepared sandwich. All around me people have been losing their footing since the day broke. My back is getting stiff from holding on to myself.

Eventually we reach a dingy, barely warm coffee shop

that has a few tables. The coffee is delicious, but the cakes and sandwiches are of a doubtful nature. Though difficult to follow when he speaks, our companion soon reveals himself to be an extreme German nationalist, a Beelzebub, who extends the ethos of the 1930s. His aggressive patriotism is alarming, as is his obsessive concern about becoming sick in Lviv.

A beggar child enters. The German instructs us not to give her money. The child, he claims, has been sent in by an adult to find out from which part of our clothing we retrieved our wallets. After we leave, he insists, we will be followed and robbed.

After lunch, we shake off our German companion and, progressing on our journey, make our way up another hill of difficulty to yet one more library, the University Library where a Mr. Kutik, the bibliographer, works. We enter and are escorted by a lady who goes to much trouble to locate him. He is found; we go upstairs to a small, chaotic office, where he sits with his hair going in all directions and his unraveling pullover creeping out from beneath his shirt. He is kind and has a wry sense of humor. He promises to help Irving if Irving returns at a certain time tomorrow; he also writes down phone numbers and contacts that might be helpful.

On the way back to our hotel, I begin to cough but think it caused by some irritant in the air. We stop at yet another restaurant pointed out by our well-meaning guide, Ihor (our *Goodwill*). I order pizza and soup. No luck. The soup tastes like a dishcloth and the pizza is an egg salad on top of dense dough. We leave and give the hotel restaurant another try. The meal is refried (I don't know how many times) chips and a cutlet.

That night it becomes apparent that I am actually sick. The following morning, I have a high fever and a wrenching cough. Ihor calls and promises to send over a doctor. While Irving pursues his research at the University Library, I stay in bed and wait until 3:00 p.m. when a doctor is supposed to arrive with a translator. At that very hour, true to the promise, there is a knock and in comes a Soviet-generation doctor: large, solid, clumsy, nice, and round-faced with instruments as old as they look and not sanitary. For this reason, I don't let her take my temperature. She listens to my chest and bronchial tubes (and takes forever), flips my breasts like pieces of rubber in and out of my bra, and then takes my blood pressure. Before leaving, she gives me a prescription (which the translator refers to as a "reception") for an antibiotic, an expectorant (which comes in a horrible-looking bottle I dread going near), a cough suppressant, and aspirin. I ache terribly and am in a bad way. I take some aspirin and wait impatiently for Irving to return. Eventually, in the early evening, he does, but I learn that because there is so much sickness in Lviv, the pharmacies have run out of the antibiotic I require. With the hope of offering me some help, the hotel manager sends a messenger to a pharmacy in another part of the city. He returns with some other antibiotic (labeled in Russian) that might help.

For over a week, I am sunk in the *Slough of Despond*. Unlike Bunyan's pilgrim, I am not able to drag myself out of the bog. While Irving pursues his search, I am lonely and despondent in this quagmire of fever. I have no means of talking to people. I am stuck with my own ignorance. Each morning, I drag myself to breakfast and leave with extra packets of soft cheese and juice so I shall have something to nourish me until evening when Irving returns.

The hotel turns off the heat during the day, so in the hope of capturing some warmth, I climb under the blanket, wrap scarves around me, and crawl into a sheepskin jacket. (I am hardly a Venus in furs.) I wait for the maids to come to the room. One housekeeper pities me and wants to make me tea. She brings in a stained cup, takes water from the tap, puts in a coil, fetches tea and sugar, and offers me a hot drink I do not have the heart to refuse. Though we do not share a language, I owe my life to her. I moan, ache, listen to books on tape (they too save my life), and try to watch television (for a few hours in the evenings, there is one static-bitten channel that shows nothing but downhill skiing—and anyway I cannot understand anything being said). I cough, sleep, and waken to hear my lungs whistling. When Irving returns, I listen to him relate his adventures and wait for him to bring me some hot food from the restaurant after he has finished eating.

During my sickness, Irving goes to mail a postcard and asks a lady he sees on the street to show him where the post-box is. After they converse in German, she invites him to her apartment so he can help her write Christmas cards to friends in America—her English is imperfect. So immersed am I in the context of this pilgrimage, my mind temptingly and ridiculously entertains thoughts of the model for the masochistic Venus in Furs, a Baroness Bogdanoff, who seduced the writer by asking him to help her improve her writing.

> Her head was wonderful in spite of the dead stony
> eyes: it was all I could see of her. She had wrapped
> her marble-like body in a huge fur, and rolled herself
> up trembling like a cat.
> —Venus in Furs, Part I

But nothing could be further from the reality. The lady is no Venus in Furs but an elegant, refined, and impoverished remnant of the Austro-Hungarian Empire, a reminder of a softer, more settled, enlightened, and affluent time. When Irving takes her to coffee, she, exhibiting her old-world manners, clings to his arm ("lest he fall"), kisses his hand, and invites him, if he should return, to stay with her.

In the various libraries we have already scouted, Irving meets even more librarians who are more than willing to help. They lead him down dark corridors, through sequestered catalog rooms, and then pause before the place where the Sacher-Masoch drawer is. But once it is opened, the librarian discovers the manuscript is not there. A great scurry. It is, she recalls, in another library, so arranges for it to be sent over. The manuscript contains three unpublished Jewish stories by Sacher-Masoch.

After a few days, in the evenings people start coming to the hotel to call upon Irving. There is, unfortunately, not the practice of announcing their presence from the downstairs desk; instead, visitors knock unannounced. At such moments, reluctant and embarrassed, I slip out of bed and try to repair myself in my mortal garments so I am respectable. I often suggest they go elsewhere to talk. On one occasion, the substantial daughter of a well-known Ukrainian writer and her well-fed husband come through the door. She has information for Irving, as well as phone numbers of Sacher-Masoch's relatives. The result is that in a few months Irving meets with the writer's grandson who tells him that Simon Weisenthal tried to reach Sacher-Masoch by holding séances. Moreover, the writer informs Irving that Marianne Faithfull is a descendant. A series of inconclusive emails with the former rock star leads nowhere.

At another time a Yiddish-speaking, elegiac elderly gentleman who knows nothing about Sacher-Masoch comes sorrowfully to our hotel room to converse with Irving who is fluent in Yiddish. (In Lviv there are few left. If reports are to be trusted, the last Yiddish-speaking resident died in May 2014.) On another night, a man who has just written a history of the Jews in Lviv calls. He tells Irving that he will be emigrating to Los Angeles the next day.

The invasion goes on and on. One dreadful evening, a crew making a film about Sacher-Masoch knocks, enters, and takes over the room. I crawl into a corner. Another night and another knock—in come Pasha and a young American woman, Katya, who is acting as his interpreter. Pasha is gangly, pale, bad-teethed, Russian-cigaretted, smart, and generous. Katya is voluble, impatient, and manic. Neither of us is sure why they come to the room, for they know little about Sacher-Masoch. Both are, however, familiar with the city and offer to take Irving on a walking tour the next day. In negative-thirty-degree Centigrade temperatures, they tour the old Jewish part of the city. (Before World War II, Jews made up over one-third of the population.) From that day on, the two do not leave us alone. It is exhausting.

After many days, I am recovered enough to leave—and we have stayed long enough.

The night before departure is New Year's Eve. Ihor, our figure of *Goodwill*, comes to bid us farewell. He keeps saying "congratulations" when I tell him I have been sick. His good intentions (incorrectly spoken) remind Irving of a librarian who, concerned about me, repeatedly reassures Irving, "It will be alright as long as Ann does *not* get better." Still more than happy to stay in bed rather than get up, on television I watch the Ukrainian president give a sober address before midnight (I do not know what he is saying); I listen to people partying in the hotel downstairs. The music continues until 6:00 a.m.; firecrackers go off during the night, and my cough hacks on.

Fuzzy-headed and armed with cheese and juice for the return trip, we go down to the hotel lobby and wait for our taxi. Pasha and Katya, who have been up all night, show up and insist on riding with us to the train station. Katya's spectacles are barely holding her eyes together; Pasha's hat and head are more angular than ever. His ever-greasy locks stick out in odd ways from under his hat. It is a good thing the two accompany us, for the taxi driver, misunderstanding our request, is mistakenly taking us to the airport. They correct him.

Silent crowds either walk around the train station's chilled waiting hall or stand watching a television perched high on an ornate balcony overlooking a once-functioning fountain. We make our way back through the darkened tunnels and walk up to an icy platform where monstrous trains spew out coal

smoke. Underneath the wagons, the spillage from the cabin toilets hangs, suspended and frozen. Pasha wants to determine whether we are waiting on the correct platform, so instead of going back to the main entrance through the tunnels, he jumps down onto the tracks and crawls under a stationary train to reach the other side. I am incredulous. Katya is becoming more and more voluble; she cannot stop talking. Before long, we are reassured we have the correct train; we climb on and find our compartment.

Another fourteen hours. This time, Irving asks the conductor for cups of tea and boiled water to fill a hot-water-bottle he has bought in Lviv. Both bring relief to my aching head. Time passes. The train moves. In the darkling of early evening, two large foxes with bushy tails stalk through crisp fields, deer gather close to farms, and a single hare bounds across the meadows' white sheets.

In contrast with where I have been, Warsaw has never looked so bright and comforting: "And behold the City shone like the Sun: the Streets also were paved with Gold, and in them walked many men, with Crowns on their heads" (*Pilgrim's Progress*.) All is dreamlike. Warsaw becomes the "Desired

Country." I even have warm and joyful thoughts about my flat in the Hotel Sokrates. The food seems heavenly, especially after a diet of smoked chicken, cheese, bread, and burned chips. I am placed under the care of the medical staff at the American embassy. I have pleurisy and pneumonia. More antibiotics, and all will be well. Within days, I return to work at the Institute of English, and life resumes. The past two weeks have been a dream—at times a nightmare.

Eventually the year is up and it is time to leave Warsaw and say farewell to Poland. Tearful Eva gives me a painting of the old town, Agata clings, and others promise to stay in touch. During the last week, minutes stretch into sad, protracted hours, yet, paradoxically, the clock speeds ahead. In the end, unable to outrun the swift passage of the remaining days, I must surrender to the inevitable and depart. Flying home, hovering between what was and what is to be, I am nowhere. In months to come, however, my experiences in Poland all too predictably bond with the past. The space between the then and the now expands; remembrances cease to trespass, tumble over, and trip up the present.

PART TWO

UKRAINE, 2000

Eastern Europe draws me once more. As difficult and surreal as the visit to Lviv five years earlier had been, my experiences there, nevertheless, had whetted my curiosity. I wanted to return, so, under the auspices of a Fulbright fellowship, I, with Irving, was off again. This time, my curiosity took me, like Alice, down the rabbit hole to other regions of Ukraine, where for a year I unlocked doors and stepped through the looking glass to gaze at the other side of things. And just in time, for later much was to change. Beginning in March 2014, Vladimir Putin destabilized the country by taking back Crimea and then by waging a proxy war, using Ukrainian separatists and "little green men." Lacking a wholehearted commitment from the West as well as adequate financial, political, and military support from its allies, Ukraine, already weakened by its oligarchs and an exploitative civil service, faltered and worried about its future.

CHAPTER 5:

A WORRIED STILLNESS

UKRAINE: FEBRUARY – MID-DECEMBER 2000

Sweeping clouds of the evening sky chase the frozen fields and soon surrender to the approaching city's sparse grid of flickering lights. The plane from London to Kiev lands. This is the last stage of a journey begun two days ago in Buffalo, New York. It is February 2000.

I have come to a Ukraine caught between its independence from the Soviet Union in 1991 and Russia's bullying return in 2014. Wedged between loyalties to the East and the West, and profoundly sobered by memories of Chernobyl and its consequences, people anxiously hold their breath and get on with life as best they can. There is a tense peace. Frustrated reactions to galloping parliamentary corruption, broken trade agreements, debates about the gas line, and an increasing national debt are audible but kept in check by the harness of political jargon and false promises. A guarded openness typifies and surrounds both the country's governmental agencies and the institutions representing Western interests. (The American Chamber of Commerce in Kiev, promoting American investment in Ukraine, is an armed fortress.)

In 2000, even though a worried stillness seems to diffuse most everything, people are ripening for the Orange Revolution of 2004, but they are not, as yet, explicitly imagining the deadly insanity of open civil conflict between Ukrainian nationalists and pro-Russian separatists, as well as competition for power among regional oligarchs. Nor is the public expecting that in thirteen years, Russian troops will march into, fight for, and seize Ukrainian territory. I have come at a time between hope and despair.

ENTRANCE

Popping noises of fluorescent bulbs accompany questions: How much money do I have with me? How many rings? Replicating my own crumpled and anxious state of mind, my travel-worn bags move through the X-ray machines and drop untidily onto the floor. Relief. The assistant from the Fulbright office is actually here to meet Irving and me. She is to drive us to a flat we have rented but never seen. On the drive to 36 Bohdan Khmelnitski in the center of Kiev, her singsong English floats like an unheard yet well-rehearsed melody from the front seat of the van to the back, where we sit numbed by both the travel and the realization that I have actually chosen to come here for a year to teach American literature in the Foreign Literature department of Taras Shevchenko University.

When the assistant drops us off in the care of Halla, a friend of our absent landlady, I feel alone, particularly since I know neither Ukrainian nor Russian. Evening falls into night. I twist the grudging front-door knob in various illogical directions and, with my booted foot, push the heavy wooden door, which leads into a pitch-black entrance hall where the smell

of urine and sounds of dripping water await whoever dares enter. Just enough light from the street lamps leaks through the smeared windowpane above the front door to expose menacing wires hanging from some electric, or perhaps telephone, apparatus attached to a flaking wall. Rusted mailboxes line another wall. Some are locked; others gape and display their neglected mouths. Ahead, my anxious eyes catch the serpentine shadows cast by a chipped marble staircase winding behind a narrow lift suitable for two and a half people.

No light switch is visible. In the months to come, I learn to carry a small flashlight with me so as to find my way down dark passageways and unfamiliar hallways. Following Halla's shadowy motions, I cautiously walk ahead and pull aside the lift's clanking metal gates, shut them, and as instructed, press button number 3. Complaining, the lift wobbles upward. Later, when visiting a friend's flat, I watch her demurely jump up and down to persuade the lift to move—a technique shared by all who live in her block.

On this first night, the lift door opens into a hall as dark as a Kiev winter night; Halla finds the light switch. My neighbors are soon quick to tell me that it is essential to turn it off immediately after use—electricity is at a minimum. Even so, I am soon to find out that we are in a privileged section of the city, for we have hot water and electricity most of the day, none of which is metered. In other areas of Kiev and throughout other cities and rural communities in Ukraine, such conveniences are available only a few hours a day (routinely between 4:00 and 6:00 p.m.) and sometimes not accessible at all, depending on the whim of either the Russians, who control the pipeline, or local district officials. Ukraine relies on Russia for half of its gas supplies. Efforts continue to locate alternatives from European providers, such as Germany, the Czech Republic, Slovakia, and Poland.

The hall light weakly illuminates the door to our apartment. Like so many in the city, this door is solid, seemingly impenetrable, made of ominous steel and padded like a vault. Feeling like Alice after she's tumbled out of her familiar world, through darkness, and landed underground in a hallway where all the doors are locked, I wander from door to door and wonder if the large key Halla has given me will admit us to our flat. Is the lock too large or too small? After I insert my key into what seems to be the right lock, the recalcitrant door to flat number 8 reluctantly gives and we are inside.

As will happen many times in the months ahead, unlit passageways and unopened doors preface entrances. A few weeks later, for instance, invited to a diplomat's flat, I open the door of his grand building and feel my way through the crumbling plaster of a dim hall. Once in, I step into a diminutive unsavory lift and reach for buttons that have lost their legibility to repetitive fingers. I am reminded of a recurring nightmare in which I attempt to make a phone call to report an emergency and find that all the numbers and letters are the same. After I randomly press a button, the doors close and the lights go out. I hastily push another button: up the elevator groans and disgorges my body onto a landing under construction. To reach the diplomat's residence, I need to go up one more flight, but as I approach the stairs a glimmer of half-light unexpectedly reveals a chasm ready to claim me as its victim (a new staircase is yet to be constructed). Unlike Alice, I am shaken and unable to think "nothing of tumbling downstairs." And never mind considering "how brave they'll all think of me at home."

Rather, I am reminded of Robert Louis Stevenson's David Balfour, who, in the blackness of a blustery Scottish night, vigilantly climbs the deteriorating steps in the tower of his murderous uncle's estate (*Kidnapped*). Horrified, David watches as sheets of lightning illuminate a sudden drop where the stairs abruptly end. He, too, knows he could have plunged to his death. I bang on the door of apartment 24 and through a speaker plead for help. A young man, who thankfully speaks English, responds, goes with me to the lift, and pushes another button. Soon I am standing outside apartment 26 where I am meant to be.

There is life beyond this prefatory darkness, for when the solidly bolted doors in these dimly lit passageways yield, they give way to lighted spaces that exist behind their forbidding opaqueness. Through these entrances, life becomes "curiouser and curiouser." I know "something *interesting* is sure to happen" when, like Alice, I lean up against a padded steel door and step through the looking-glass that "has got all soft like gauze," so I can travel to the other side and see things "the other way." Sometimes the dark squalor of the hallway reverses itself to become a spacious, bright, and even luxurious set of rooms. Behind the diplomat's impermeable door, sunlit spaces with gleaming parquet floors covered in rugs from Kazakhstan dazzle me. I admire a splendid bathroom and a solidly made balcony from which one looks over Kiev and watches the evening sun descend over the city's hills.

On the first night, I step through my own steel door into a far less luxurious flat, but I do find light, fifteen-foot ceilings, a study with extensive airy windows, a bright kitchen, antique cabinets filled with fine bone china, and in a long, large elegant living room, an out-of-tune concert grand piano the landlady has tucked into a corner. The music of Chopin and Schubert lies scattered and opened on its lid. Our landlady, Luba Zuk, grew up in Ukraine and is a professor of piano at McGill University. Her brother, Ireneus, who is also a musician, often comes to Kiev to perform and teach.

Inside, "cats become bats," and "bats become cats." The shower sprays sideways, rather than down, the telephone does not speak, and, worst of all, the bed is not a bed. Halla explains that the better "bed" is in the living room—it's a sofa that pushes down to make a single bed. The other option is a narrow sofa, which does not open up, in the study. We try to lie on the one in the living room, but the mattress, consisting of three hard pillows, slopes on one side and, on the other, cuts one's body into some sort of triptych. Months later, we finally walk two miles down Bohdan Khmelnitski to a large department store with creaky wooden floors and thieves. Armed with the right measurements, we find a mattress ($30), wrap string around it, clumsily haul it down three flights of marble stairs, lug it outside to a taxi stand, and go home where we squish ourselves and it into the unwilling lift, step on a resident's foot, and eventually heave our salvation onto the sofa—all in an hour's time.

YELENA

The morning after our arrival, I hear an insistent ringing of the doorbell. I open the door to find Yelena Abromowich. Her generous body is held together by an apron, smeared with a lifetime of cooking. A maternal smile stretches across a face rutted and left raw by love, death, and care. When she greets me in enthusiastic Russian, her frizzled hair sputters close to her timeworn eyes. Linguistically inept, I am helpless and retreat from the swollen feet moving toward me. I call Irving, who speaks the language. Determined to communicate with me, Yelena persists, even though I can neither respond nor understand. Later, if I manage to articulate one or two Ukrainian or Russian phrases, she assumes that I am miraculously fluent and exuberantly fires away in an increasingly loud voice. I am frustrated with myself.

Yelena lives in the adjoining flat. Our landlady told her that we would be there. For the next few months, she repeatedly rings the doorbell (sometimes several times a day and often before we are awake in the morning). She adopts us and supplements her meager income by doing our laundry by hand. It always comes back ironed and folded—even the underwear.

Two or three times a week, she also cooks for us. Yelena is Jewish and knows Irving is too, so week after week, she brings helpings of kasha, homemade gefilte fish, beetroot salad, borscht, and homemade cherry preserves. For me, she brings cookies. The food is good but I cannot help but notice that it arrives in dishes with bits of the previous meal still on them. We taste the wine made from grapes growing on vines that reach up to her third-floor balcony above the busy street and pavement below. She and her husband planted the vine years ago and waited for it to reach their balcony. Later I will learn that this practice is not uncommon—here, the city is often transformed into a subsistence farm. In poorer areas of Kiev, people grow vegetables, keep chickens, and tether goats on their city apartment balconies.

One morning, dressed in her gaping slip and a loosely knitted woolen pullover Irving gave her, Yelena rings the bell, plants a big wet kiss on my cheek, and like the Duchess in *Alice*, affectionately rests her chin on my shoulder. She wants me to see her apartment. It is twice the size of ours. In her kitchen, a pet yellow finch is out of its cage and pecking away at a loaf of bread. It flutters over and perches on a massive sausage sprawled on the kitchen table. With great pride, Yelena leads me into a large bedroom dominated by an equally large, pink satin-covered bed on which she has arranged her dolls for me to admire. Deprived of a real bed, I long to lie on it.

I go into her flat only one more time, in April, for a seder during Passover, a holiday that Irving, though not religious, is eager to observe, particularly in a place where these rituals risk erasure. He is full of expectation. But, of course, we are behind the looking glass and much is the reverse of what it is supposed to be.

We sit down to dinner with Yelena, her husband, their grown-sorrowful son, and another neighbor, who is a retired biologist and also Jewish. He looks ninety but is only sixty-six years old. He, like Yelena and her husband, survived, somehow, the various persecutions accompanying the Nazi occupation of Kiev. They returned to Kiev after the war and are now among one hundred thousand Jews who are said to live in the city.

Irving has come to the seder with his yarmulke on and a Haggadah tucked under his arm so he might lead the ritual. He tries to read the four questions, but no one knows anything about them or seems to be interested, perhaps with the exception of the retired biologist. During Irving's attempts, the television, which was already on, receives more attention. Yelena and her husband keep twisting their necks to catch a glimpse of the latest crisis taking place on the soap opera, and the son talks with tears in his eyes about how his cat waits for him and how he sings to his cat.

Suddenly the table bursts into a Yiddish wedding song, and, after more vodka fuels that melody, the son, in a lovely tenor voice, warbles a popular tune. Then the biologist speaks about how much TV ruins culture and how hard his life is. Giving up, Irving closes the Haggadah and puts it well aside to make room for the photograph album Yelena places on the table. I look at black-and-white snapshots of her with her first two husbands, the first of whom was killed when a plane crashed on their apartment building. I see a younger Yelena, unembarrassedly spilling out of her bikini, and I see her first husband hugging their crippled daughter. In the midst of all this, the doorbell rings; a neighbor from upstairs anxiously inquires if her missing parrot has flown in through Yelena's window. The dinner collapses.

Like the neighbor's parrot, the rituals and memories of Judaism have taken wing, leaving behind a few tattered feathers of remembrance that congregate in obscure murky corners of the city. With the possible exception of two splendid Moorish-style synagogues, to be renovated after we leave (one has metamorphosed into an ammunition dump, the other into a puppet theater), leftovers of a time when Judaism flourished lie damaged and sequestered waiting to be resuscitated by a gust of fresh wind. A specially organized three-hour bus tour of Jewish Kiev promises to give a glimpse of what remains. With a large group of elderly Jews who have emerged from their underground spaces, I board a crowded bus. Jammed into a seat for what seems an eternity, I see nothing except the huddled shoulders of the people seated in front of me and the thickly coated standing bodies packed into the bus's narrow aisles. My view is blocked, and I am left staring at the crudely woven fabric of the seat cover before me. A static Ukrainian commentary, sputtering through a dysfunctional microphone, completes the obstruction.

Days later, a quest to find the site of Babi Yar (Old Wives Ravine) on the outskirts of Kiev is equally elusive. In 1941, thousands of Jews, who had been rounded up and sent on a forced march from the city center, were lined up, shot, and pitched over into this ravine. None of our acquaintances is sure where it is, not even those who are supposed to know, such as Nellie, a Jewish professor of philology, who attempts to assist us. When we seem close to where she thinks the memorial is, the torn, ragged earth of a construction site for a new metro subway stop foils our futile search. Remembrances of a Jewish past are being driven below levels of visibility and consciousness.

Yiddish, which once reverberated through the streets of nineteenth-century Kiev, has also gone underground, muted and almost forgotten. Rummaging among the few remaining voices, Irving and I go in search of the only Jewish center—located, we are told, down a quiet side street not far from where we live. We approach and find neither sign nor nameplate. Hoping we have come to the right place, we walk through a foreboding archway leading downward to a gloomy passage, then out to a dreary courtyard in which a parched, forlorn fountain waits for life-giving water to articulate its thoughts. Shut doors bar our way; we crank one open, go down steps, meet another padded steel entrance, and buzz to be admitted. After descending yet another shadowed stairwell, we emerge into a newly painted basement in which low ceilings almost prevent us from standing up. I am disappointed not to see the White Rabbit rushing through. Instead, I catch sight of a dwindling collection of sedentary elderly people, wrapped in their coats and thick stockings to keep warm. It is a Yiddish group run by a man who is hard of hearing and does not seem to catch anything anyone says. Among those few present, Yiddish, Ukrainian, and Russian, as well as the local hybrid of Ukrainian and Russian idioms battle for attention and stumble over each other. A stout woman, weighed down by both her galoshes and a heavily knitted beret that deflates the bouffant curls of her hair, interrupts the cacophonous confusion and approaches an upright piano. She begins playing (beautifully) a Chopin nocturne. For the moment the piece's melancholic, sweet harmony dissipates the dissonance of the gathering. A few bars in, however, the deaf leader abruptly gets to his feet and loudly proclaims, "That's not Jewish; play something Jewish!" ("Off with her head!") The next day, the man calls and apologizes for the ragged meeting.

There are to be many Mad Hatter tea parties. The seder and the Yiddish group preface our own. At the end of May, Irving organizes a party in our flat. The usual arguments ensue about how many and whom to invite. Irving likes to have many people and mix various strata of his life, while I prefer to have fewer. The problem begins the day before when we go through an underground passage where a bedraggled young street musician plays passages from Vivaldi and Bach on an accordion. Irving stands star struck before him. Over my stern but impotent disapproval, he hands the musician our address and asks him to come and play at our party. When he shows up at the door, my Ukrainian friends have a fit, for they fear he is a bandit and will rob us all.

The relaxed pleasure of the gathering disappears. My friends anxiously retreat to the kitchen and wonder what to do next—it is all a riddle to them. Our neighbors sit nervously in the living room at one end of the table so they can consume most of the food before he takes it all. Unlike the Mad Hatter's tea party, nobody either changes places or moves down a seat. All are frozen. After a while, Irving gives the accordionist a shot of brandy; soon the Vivaldi is "looped" or unseasonable, certainly not as mellifluous as it had seemed to be in the underground passage. Upset, people leave earlier than they should have.

The following day Tamara, Natalia, and Yelena call to see if we are alive. We are, but not without some discomfort, for after they departed, leaving their worried looks hanging on the hallstand, the young man drank more and more brandy, asked to spend the night, slumped into the cushions of our bed-sofa, and, like the dormouse, went off into a doze. Time did not move for him, nor did it for those of us left to endure his unsettling presence. I wished, like Alice, that I could pinch him and he would go. Ellie, an American friend from years ago, was still there. Speaking fluent Ukrainian she came to the rescue and gently, but firmly, maneuvered him out of the door. Before he left, he handed Irving a stolen Rolex watch. Irving, like the Mad Hatter, did not know what to do with it. He looked at it uneasily, shaking it every now and then, and held it to his ear. I went to bed thinking, as did Alice, that it was "the stupidest tea-party I ever was at in all my life."

ROOM 73

In the morning, the hands of time move again, and, as on most days, I continue to traverse dark passages and open locked doors. The door to room 73 (the Department of Foreign Literature) in the humanities building of Taras Shevchenko University is one that still haunts my waking. This room *is* the department. Everything takes place here, for no one has an office. To reach it, I pass through a once-splendid, yawning hall where students, carrying their plastic folders, drift in and out of consciousness in the half-light of early risings, and where, in a shadowed corner, a woman sells lukewarm tea and sparkling ruby-jam tarts that tempt the starved eye.

Stretching before me, a marble staircase leads to upper floors inhabited by echoing corridors and locked entrances. After coming to room 73, I knock and enter. Inside, the veneer of a long mahogany table, left over from a more affluent time, reflects what light steals through a set of windows. Around the table, mismatched chairs rearrange themselves to suit the needs of the moment. Bookcases and piles of papers line the walls, and off to the side, Luba the secretary, relegated to a worn wooden desk, sits before a manual typewriter that, whenever she uses it, threatens to upset an electric water heater perched close by.

Luba exudes a comforting, matronly presence, but, unfortunately, I cannot communicate with her. When I am alone with her and need something, I dash into the hall to find a student (most of whom know English) who can translate for me. The linguistic abilities of the younger generation are extraordinary; for them, knowing a foreign tongue is a way out, a passport to elsewhere, perhaps to a job with a multinational. In spite of the requirement that courses be taught in Ukrainian, the university is a babble of tongues, a multilingual world. My students are fluent not only in English but also in other languages, and many in the art of simultaneous translation. One of my students, in fact, is periodically absent from lectures because she is the translator for the government's commission to Holland. The dean of the humanities division is President Kushma's personal interpreter. Even the young woman who meticulously cuts my hair spends her free hours poring over what few texts she can afford that give her practice in English. (She hopes to find an American husband.)

My colleagues are scattered about room 73. One senior professor and former chair, who writes about James Joyce and studies Austrian literature, casts a skeptical, forbidding eye. Wearing close-fitting black leather pants and holding a cigarette between the taut tips of her fingers, Keera leans against an open window in order to expel the smoke and her thoughts into the Kiev sky. Upon my arrival, she turns and nods but does not speak. (Months later, she utters her first words to me when she inquires where my pants are—I have been wearing slacks all winter to protect my legs from the cold, but on this day, I have decided to wear a skirt. Meekly, I cite the coming of warmer weather. Later, she engages me in a mixture of Hungarian, German, and English.)

In another part of the room, Tamara, who specializes in American literature, tutors a postgraduate. As she bends over the student's paper, her thinning henna hair falls limply over the cascade of her generosity. During this session, Tamara's commitment to her work and her enthusiasm for her subject rejuvenate her face and defy the indelible marks of woe and age that lie beneath the morning's mask of heavily applied powder and smudged eyeliner. Together, they speak Ukrainian.

At the other end of the table, Victoria and Lydia, under the watchful eye of their senior professor, obediently tutor students. Next to them, one of the many Olgas I am to know underlines sentences in a book of literary criticism sent to her by an acquaintance in America, a corn farmer from Iowa who cares nothing for things literary but remembers her fondly. Later, over coffee at a nearby café, I step into the mire of cultural and linguistic differences and struggle to reach some firmer ground where I might better understand a colleague's thoughts about the meaning of feminism. I am not sure I succeed.

Eventually my attention turns to a drab, middle-aged figure in brown. Propped by a bulging, worn briefcase, Natalia stands determinedly erect beneath a prominently displayed framed photograph of her father, who founded the department fifty years ago. (The briefcase was once his.) Beaming through the shadow cast by the paternal portrait, she advances to greet me. From that moment on, she affectionately yet authoritatively directs my life (as she does others'). Every day, she phones to see how I am. In time, I grow dependent on her attention and her will. Only once do I foolishly attempt to resist her iron resolve, when through the Fulbright's generosity, I purchase, from the States, $3,000 of recent critical studies to be put in the bookcases of room 73. The dearth of such books in the various university libraries is conspicuous. As a result, whenever it is financially feasible, my colleagues travel, via grants, to literary conferences in Moscow to acquire what is unavailable in Kiev.

I purchase these books so that the foreign literature students and professors will be able to take one or two from the shelves whenever curiosity or need dictates. However, that is not to be, for as soon as the books arrive and are set in place, Natalia, ready and waiting, with a key held tightly between her thumb and index finger, resolutely locks the bookcases' glass doors. No one, she instructs, may open these without her permission. The books, as well as my hopes, are firmly impounded.

For days, a battle of wills ensues. Ineffectively, I argue that students and colleagues should be free to look at them, even, heaven forbid, check them out. Frustrated, I try to devise some makeshift system for their circulation. Like Medusa ready to turn me to stone, Natalia glares back, shakes the coiled plaits circling her head, and refuses. I persist and persist, but to no avail. I lose. Since no shield of Perseus materializes to deflect her gaze, the best I can do is convince the secretary to let me sit down at her machine and type a list of the contents so the inhabitants of room 73 might have some idea of what is impounded behind the glass. While I obstinately (perhaps annoyingly) tap the keys, Natalia glares immovable on a chair next to me. That bibliography, I am sure, now lies forgotten and unread in the dark recesses of the secretary's bottom drawer. Is it the fear of theft; is it the wish to maintain a hierarchy that privileges the professor over the student; is it a sense of professional competition that wants to take possession of ideas so that only they have access to them; or is it the value of the books themselves? I never know, but I think it the last. I do know, however, that my colleagues, like dogs with a bone, keep to themselves their books purchased abroad. Once more, cultural difference muddies my understanding, and I fail to reach solid footing.

A paradox of immobility and innovation, Natalia, however, through her sheer willpower, opens many more doors than she closes. Wanting to make use of my "expertise" and reform the department's academic program, she requires the students to alter their regular programs and spend time with me. She bends the rigid structures of the traditional curriculum (in the interest of nation building, Russian literature must be read in Ukrainian) so as to erect a more malleable scaffolding to support the courses she wishes me to teach. As a result, while I am there, foreign literature students from each year are required to take multiple eight-week units on African American women writers, minority literature, surveys of modern American literature, and special sessions on individual writers, such as Thoreau. Throughout, I offer supplemental materials through videos, photographs, and tapes I have brought with me. Because the library holdings in American literature and culture are so weak (the American Institute library has more books on business practices than on literature and culture) students have a chance to see materials that are otherwise unavailable, except perhaps through special television programs.

Used to obediently listening and taking notes, most of these students do not question what I say. Even when encouraged, they prefer, as they have been taught, to absorb information and not, in public at least, ask critical or challenging questions. That is the way. Yet that habit in class does not mean that they are not thinking. I come to realize this when Natalia makes it possible for thirty students from other departments to take a seminar on Ralph Ellison's *Invisible Man*. Having read every word, they come voluntarily every week to discuss two chapters at a time. A

faculty member of the Linguistic University occasionally partic-
ipates. Because we are moving slowly through this complex text,
spaces for spoken thought and searching questions open up. I
sometimes wonder if my students at times also feel invisible.
But even Natalia, bolstered by her heritage and her briefcase, cannot always rise above the vindictive and obstreperous
world that surrounds her. Occasionally she collapses, and the
tightly bound Ukrainian plats that circle her forehead loosen
ever so slightly. Once after making a major scheduling error,
Natalia fleetingly displays a fragile vulnerability. Painfully
embarrassed, she lists what else has gone wrong in the last
twenty-four hours: she has smashed her glasses and must now
read with an old pair enhanced by a magnifying glass; moreover, she has spilled red-current jam on her blouse and spent
hours scrubbing it off. Natalia, as do all of my colleagues, has
few clothes and has learned in childhood how to clean wools
without the benefit of dry cleaning. Dry-cleaning establish-
ments are costly and are labeled "American."

The people of room 73 earn the equivalent of a meager
$40 per month—that is, if they get paid. There are dry periods,
which they must frugally and stoically endure as well as supple-
ment with other work. Olga, Victoria, Lydia, Yelena, Natalia,
and Tamara teach courses at other universities, earn extra cash
by working at foreign embassies or by translating for corpo-
rations headquartered in Kiev—one translates American car-
toons and comic strips for Ukrainian media, and another edits
a magazine for Ukrainian Airlines. Most of these women live
alone and support their grown struggling daughters who, suffering from health problems after the Chernobyl disaster and
because of economic hardship, have never left home. The men
have absconded and started other lives with unnamed women,
never to be heard from again.

Under Natalia's watchful reign, room 73 is a matriarchy of
dedication and determination, except occasionally when an elderly

professorial male enters its domain. Then the power of the matriarchy either withers into obsequiousness (such as the time a gentlemanly Hungarian wanders in or when Irving gives a paper and Natalia literally applauds each thought) or deteriorates into vitriolic whisperings (such as the day the university rector, attempting to unseat Natalia, appoints a male favorite to the department faculty). Equilibrium returns only when the culprit blunders back through the door and that door firmly closes to keep at bay the ineradicable dye of patriarchal authority staining the corridors.

Corruption also stalks these halls. In the university system, it is not uncommon for students, particularly an increasing number who are "private"—paying their own fees, not admitted through competitive exams, and hence not supported by the government—to pay a bribe for a degree. But not so in room 73 where my colleagues tutor, reexamine, and spend many extra hours with all their charges until their students legitimately pass the exit examination and papers.

Classroom space is limited. As a result, my seminar-style classes must meet in room 73. Frustrating my attempts to fathom the pure waters and depths of Walden Pond, a surfeit of humanity in the room sullies and disturbs the quiet, lyrical passages from Thoreau's *Walden* that the students read on worn Xeroxed sheets. Around me, the room's usual activities persist unapologetically. Coming and going, colleagues boil water for cups of tea, hang up coats, take off boots, drape wet clothes on the radiator, prepare notes, and gossip. The telephone's repetitive ring, the click of the typewriter keys, the *ch-ch-ch* overtones of whispering Ukrainian voices, and the opening and closing of the door, as well as the roar of endless traffic rising from the cobbled street below, drown my words and, from time to time, plunge me into despair, in spite of the students' receptiveness to the text. Afterwards, I escape and purchase an espresso at a nearby hotel, which also has the benefit of a clean toilet. The bathroom close to room 73 is an old-style hole, smudged and reeking.

The same struggle to keep my words afloat is true when I move to the British Language Center Library next door. In the midst of a class on *Invisible Man*, students walk through and chatter as if I too were imperceptible. Sometimes I try to read there but inevitably I am once more interrupted—this time by an overly eager colleague from another department, whom in all honesty I would rather avoid. She dashes in to see me. I am horrified to notice that her face is splotched a pale green and her hair a bright orange. She fell while rushing from the university to another appointment and has just gotten out of hospital. Like a cartoon figure, she now sees stars in her eyes.

Yelena, the kind librarian of the British Language Center, tries her best to help, but she too lives in a world of small spaces and noisy clutter. One afternoon I phone her at home but cannot hear a thing she says because of her barking dog. Yelena later explains that she has not only a dog but also a very large puppy whose eager face can rest on a tabletop. Moreover, she owns a cat and a three-month-old kitten. Pandemonium breaks out when the puppy accidentally sits down on the kitten and there is a rush to rescue it. Naively, I ask, "How many rooms are there in the apartment in which you, your husband, and all these animals live?"

"One," she replies.

THE UNIVERSITY LIBRARY

Seeking respite from this disorder and in quest of a quiet, spacious setting, I periodically cross the street to the university library, a grand nineteenth-century yellow building that promises silence and space. Oak catalog cabinets stuffed with fading index cards either tilt exhausted in muted corridors or congregate aimlessly in silent side rooms. A curtained space in the gaping, drafty lobby conceals a single Xerox machine (difficult to find elsewhere, particularly functioning ones that do not muddle the paper or print blank pages). A young woman works the machine. I become friendly with her. Wanting an escape from her dead-end life, she conscientiously studies English and practices on me. One day in tears, she tells me that her mother (probably trying to do her best) is pressuring her to break up with her boyfriend and sign up for a marriage bureau that links girls with American men (hopefully rich ones). These men come over for a few days, pick up a bride, and take her home—to who knows what.

Leaning toward her, I urge her to continue to resist her mother's wishes and offer to put her in touch with an organization that might give support. I wonder where she is now. Later, alone with a couple in a funicular on its long way down from Mount Ai-Petri (4,500 feet) in Crimea, I listen to a conversation between a plaid-shirted, potbellied, middle-aged Midwesterner and a thin, blond, desperate Ukrainian woman who replies in broken English. An agency has obviously just linked them up, for there is no real intimacy. Invisible, for they think I am Ukrainian and know no English, I eavesdrop as the man speaks of their future life in suburban America. His words reverberate through the descending compartment and sound out with a controlling timbre that will manage her life if she stays with him—a power probably no longer available to him at home. Her only response is "I vant a little doggie"—a request he promptly stomps on and kills by saying "No, I wouldn't allow that!" She pleads again. Unhappily, he mutters that he would have to think about it and then quickly shoots back, "When we have children, you won't need a dog." (It is obvious to me that this woman is past childbearing age.)

I feel sick and fantasize that I should interrupt and tell her to get out before it is too late. But dangling in midair and feeling vulnerable myself, I fail. She will find her way to America, but what then?

Upstairs in the university library, I open the door to a large reading area and discover a moderately well-lit place where the daylight peers through a row of tightly shut windows and where flickering fluorescent bulbs articulate their imminent demise with rhythmic popping sounds. Conscientious students wearing coats, gloves, and scarves bend wordlessly over their work at rows of desks. The feeble warmth from the radiators is useless in this vacuous space. As if darkly impersonating a pompous Mr. Bumble in charge of the workhouse in *Oliver Twist*, a librarian oversees these students from an elevated platform at the head of the room. Afraid to ask for anything, I quietly choose a place and start my work. An imposing portrait of Kushma (the president of Ukraine), replete with medals, lends weight to the librarian's rule. All seems to go well until the librarian rises and with guttural severity gives a strict command, which, of course, I do not understand. Everyone obediently leaves the room; puzzled, I follow their lead.

Like a lost soul, I wait, exiled and wondering, in the dark hall. Eventually, the doors reopen, and with the other expelled readers I start to file back in. The room, however, is far colder than before. The fragile heat, which dared an hour or so ago to try to do battle with a biting cold that intermittently charged the room's shut windows, is now defeated. Gusts of icy air advance through gaping panes of glass, which have been opened wide during our absence. What has happened? Believing it necessary periodically to rid the room of germs as well as of foul particles, the librarian, following official policy, clears the room twice a day, opens all the windows for a long fifteen minutes (no matter what the temperature outside), and shuts them again before readmitting us. Once a pale, strained, and puzzled face follows me out and asks what on earth is going on. She is an American postgraduate student studying Ukrainian literature. I explain, and she answers that she has had enough culture shock for one day and is going back to her apartment. I never see her again.

In time, I grow used to this procedure and occasionally even welcome it when yesterday's onions join a lingering troop of body odors and march around the room in search of a billet. I feel comfortable here—that is, except for the time I choose a desk next to a window looking over a concrete courtyard behind the university hospital. Indulging a morbid state of mind, I distractedly watch nurses and white-jacketed attendants come and go between the backdoor of the hospital and a hulking garbage container to the left of the window. They carry bulging white plastic bags (with human parts—the casualties of battle? I wonder).

This impulse to clear out a room so as to cleanse the air is not only for the benefit of asthmatics (I am told) but also a vestige of the Chernobyl accident. Since April 1986, all public buildings have been annually decontaminated. Nearly fifteen years later, Chernobyl haunts people's minds and bodies (everyone has his or her own narrative), especially when symptoms of some unspecified chronic illness periodically compromise their health or when news of the now-dead village (people also mourn the loss of a culture specifically associated with that village) and pictures of the contaminated area's once-cultivated fields or wild woods periodically make the headlines or fill the television screen.

One spring afternoon, I, too, am haunted. While I conduct a class in room 73, my attention drifts to the open windows. Time passes. The sky thickens as a yellowish-green fog lowers its heavy head, crawls over tree limbs, obliterates the budding leaves, smothers the street, and swirls uninvited into the room. People dart from their chairs and slam the windows shut. Class comes to an end. Natalia tells me to go home, but says nothing more.

When I leave the building, people on the streets, like "the pestilence-stricken multitudes" in Shelley's "Ode to the West Wind," seem driven like "ghosts from an enchanter fleeing, / Yellow and black, and pale, and hectic red." Something, I worry, has happened at Chernobyl, but the wind this time, rather than blowing north, is heading straight for Kiev. On my way back to 36 Bohdan Khmelnitski, I remember a recurring dream I used to have in the 1960s, in which I was trying to outrun the radioactive dust from a nuclear bomb; now, it has left the darkened eyes of my sleep and become part of my waking. *Is this really happening? Has Chernobyl caught fire again?* I try to let the thoughts pass.

Our neighbor, Yelena, rushes into the apartment and says that "because of the strong winds," we must shut our windows. This directive puzzles me, for a fortnight earlier she accused me of not opening the windows as much as I should. Believing there is another disaster, she, in her kindly, bumbling way, is attempting to protect us from contamination.

Several hours later the fog dissipates; Natalia phones to explain that Kiev has been in a state of panic. Furies from the past have been gusting across the city and its damaged lives. The thickly menacing air, however, was not the result of an explosion at the reactor but the consequence of strong and angry fires blazing in the bogs surrounding Chernobyl. To quell fears, cabinet ministers repeatedly make announcements on the radio and appear on television programs featuring vivid pictures of the conflagration. Moreover, officials at the American embassy issue moderately reassuring statements declaring that after testing, the level of radiation in Kiev has not risen significantly.

When I am later in Belarus, a country mapped in swatches of red to mark areas affected by radiation, people nervously ask me about the incident. As always, traumatic memory clings tenaciously to consciousness. In Kiev, there is a museum devoted to the Chernobyl disaster. Natalia takes me there, though she says that she does not need a museum to remind her of that time. In addition to the gruesome, horrific exhibition of fetuses deformed by radiation and preserved in bottles for all to see, two videos in that museum stay with me. One, taken by the KGB, is of the town within the thirty-kilometer circumference surrounding the reactor. The footage is from the very day of the explosion, a few hours after, but before people are told to evacuate (of course, too late). One sees inhabitants going quite normally about their business for the last time in their lives. Another video is of volunteer "cleanup" crews, who, with inadequate protection, shortly after the explosion went into the reactor for one and a half minutes each in order to reach what machines could not. Death is their companion.

KIEV THROUGH THE LOOKING GLASS

I am embarrassed to admit that, before I came, I was not properly acquainted with alternative spellings of place names. Months earlier in London, I received the official letter informing me that I would be teaching at Taras Schevchenko University in "Kyiv." Fearing I might have been assigned to some isolated, polluted, ugly industrial city, I wandered the corridors of the Department of Slavic Studies at the University of London and roused a professor, who responding to my knock on his office door, gently assured me that "Kyiv" is the Ukrainian-Russian spelling for "Kiev." Relief: I was to spend the next year in one of the most splendid cities in Eastern Europe.

Time continues to pass, and doors to other unfamiliar places continue to open. Kiev is an active cultural city. A few yards from my flat is the magnificent nineteenth-century opera house with its expansive entrance (one imagines the grand carriages that once stood outside), and within easy reach are other theaters and symphony halls. When one goes through these buildings' looking-glass doors, the routines of a hurried, crowded, sometimes-cacophonous life reverse. For the moment, the anxieties inhabiting room 73 or 36 Bohdan Khmelnitski succumb to the fantasies of another time and transport me to another place. Often at the last minute, after surviving the crush of the cloak room (one brings a plastic bag in which to put one's boots, hat, gloves, and scarves) and paying as little as forty cents, at most five dollars, per ticket, I seek consolation from the day in the melodrama of opera (there are frequently three different operas performed per week), in the fluidity of the ballet (dancers move like water over ice), and in the intricate harmonies of orchestral music.

The reversals in this looking-glass world occasionally do more, however, than offer a pleasant and stimulating reprieve from the business of the working world. Sometimes they quite literally, absurdly, and disturbingly turn upside down and inside out what one is in the habit of knowing and assuming. As if anticipating the terrible reversals of 2013 and 2014, as well as the destabilization of Ukraine's contested borders, realities and boundaries shift to undermine or threaten one's orientation. One is sometimes at war with oneself. The familiar categories of being scatter and leave one unsettled. Alice, as she does at the conclusion of *Through the Looking-Glass*, sweeps away the tablecloth to create a jumble of things and leaves all in confusion. Order and classification no longer hold.

One week I attend a serious and moving production of *La Traviata*. The seat, a hard chair in a theater box suspended precariously over stage right, is less than perfect. This location gives me not only sore knees but also an unusual view of the performance. In the midst of a tragic scene, when the beautiful, unjustly wronged heroine is dying, the entire trombone and trumpet sections decide to have a deliriously funny time in the orchestra pit. The trumpet player, while pulling ridiculous faces, tweets the mustache of his colleague, and, in chorus, members of the trombone section stand mischievously and start running in place, pretending they are going to be late for their grand orchestral entrance in the final scene. While the conductor seems blithely to ignore these high jinks, the pudgy oboist, waiting for his entrance, shuffles around the pit in his slippers; in the wings, a tenor picks his nose. Such are the reversals of the sublime. Humpty Dumpty falls off the wall.

The opera house raises its curtains to other absurdities

that topple expectations and tilt perspective so that what seems up is really down. While absorbed in a serious moment in *Rigoletto*, I become aware of people giggling inappropriately around me. Soon the entire audience collapses in laughter. What is happening? The leading tenor has become ill and has been replaced by an understudy, who knows the libretto *only* in Ukrainian and *not* in Italian. Like battering rams, his Ukrainian vocalizations pummel the fluid syllables of the Italian lines and annihilate the tragic, lyrical timbre of the remaining moments.

Another reversal occurs when I attend what I think is going to be a splendid performance of Bach's *St. Matthew's Passion* (said to be the first in Kiev for eighty years). Anticipating a splendid performance of a more-than-splendid work, I buy a ticket from a scalper (the event is "sold out") and rush into the opera house. I arrive in the dark just as the curtain is going up. As the evening progresses, I sense that something is amiss: the oratorio is staged. The orchestra is not up to par; the soloists are uneven; and, worse, the chorus, dancers, and Roman soldiers are dressed as if they have stepped out of a horrid Sunday-school painting.

The performance really deteriorates when it comes time for the betrayal and the crucifixion. Judas sports dreadlocks; red and white lights flash; painted clouds move across a rumbling, darkened sky; and a soprano, who nearly forgets her entrance, hurries onto the stage. Moving to the front, an oversized luminous cross precedes dancers propelled by angel wings. Hauling a bible larger than a tabletop, members of the chorus follow. In the grand finale, church members mingle onstage. Thankfully, the house lights go up. I hear snippets of English around me and realize, to my embarrassment, that I am in the midst of evangelical missionaries who have dumped Bach into the wastes of the Bible Belt. Caught in a trap sprung by my nonexistent linguistic skills, I am ensnared by my inability to read the program. (At least Alice could read the labels on the bottles that took her in and out of doors.) It is a relief to exit and get back onto the street.

Later, I learn that the missionary population in Kiev is significantly large. It has money, influence, and, unfortunately, the backing of at least two foreign embassies. At this event, I am disappointed to catch sight of the wife of the US ambassador as well as the British ambassador himself.

There are to be even more twists and reversals, but not all of them are either absurd or discouraging. Instead, they are curiously wonderful. One evening, I attend a performance presented by the visiting Bolshoi Ballet. Enchanted I follow the lithe, elegant movements of the then-seventy-five-year-old Maya Plisetskaya. Once famous for her revolutionary approach to classical ballet, she continues to dance with the troupe. Her motions flow from the spring of her enduringly muscular body to defy her age. Behind this theater's looking-glass door, age becomes youth.

On another occasion, behind yet another door, youth metamorphoses into age. One early evening, I walk several miles in order to be present at the finals of the Horowitz Piano Competition for young pianists. The symphony hall is packed. After a performance given by the third- and second-place winners, a child from a godforsaken, depressed part of eastern Ukraine, who has won the competition and is just a few days from her eighth birthday, approaches the piano. Veronica Rogachova's feet barely meet the pedals. Behind her, the Kiev Philharmonic Orchestra sits and waits to accompany her. Dressed in her freshly ironed, girlish frock, a satin bow crowning her hair, she appears young and vulnerable. But when the moment comes and she confidently turns to the orchestra, nods her directive to begin, and renders the opening passages of Bach's F Minor Piano Concerto, all is utterly, utterly changed. The memory still sends shivers down my spine. In that instant, her childish features vanish. Discarding the chubbiness of childhood, her face deepens to display the shadows and authority that can accompany adulthood and that should not yet be hers; some deeper soul rises through the soft, yet-to-be-sculpted tissue of youth to furrow her brow and tighten the skin. She takes command of the music, the piano, and the orchestra (she is conducting from where she sits). Her phrasing and her subtlety are exquisite and moving—beyond the emotional boundaries of her youth. Everyone sits silent and transfixed.

Ireneus, the brother of our landlord and one of the judges, says she is a "genius" and that there is a tug-of-war over her: Moscow is trying to get her to come and study there, and the music academy in Kiev is making offers to keep her in Ukraine. Still stunned on my way back to 36 Bohdan Khmelnitski, I unexpectedly find myself walking behind her. Close to her mother's side and holding an immense teddy bear given as a prize, she skips nonchalantly along the pavement. Another metamorphosis: she has reverted to being a child again. It is too much for me.

In other theater spaces in this looking-glass world, gender reverses its supposedly stable text to create puzzling and curious fictions in which masculinity and femininity are as fluid as the gracefully choreographed movements onstage. At the Ukrainian National Theatre, men become women when an all-male ballet company, visiting from St. Petersburgh, performs *Swan Lake*. Wearing tutus and up on pointe, the company's male dancers transform themselves into a delicate corps of cygnets—into a chorus of frail femininity—and perform the principal female roles. Once in a while, a fleeting glimpse or a shadow of a masculine feature, beneath the makeup and whisping feathers, threatens to interfere and sacrifice the troupe's translation to the language of "camp." Perplexed, the audience is not sure whether to titter or not. Respectful and enchanted by the metamorphosis, however, it refuses. Later, when one holds the extraordinary evening up to a mirror, it is difficult to read the performance's text. The more one tries to make sense, the more one becomes entangled in, perhaps attracted to, the puzzle.

> *'Twas brillig, and the slithy toves*
> > *Did gyre and gimble in the wabe:*
> *All mimsy were the borogoves,*
> > *And the mome raths outgrabe.*

—"Jabberwocky"

A similar enigma follows me when we spend a weekend in Riga (Latvia). I am excited to enter the recently renovated and gilded opera house to attend a classical recital performed by a popular and well-known alto singer. Having walked all day through the old city and filled up on pastries bought at the Lido, Irving and I quickly change into polite clothes and make our way past posters announcing the concert. A bit puzzled, we look at the publicity photograph and see that the soloist has none of the dramatic flair of a prima donna. She wears a turtleneck sweater that struggles to ascend her three double chins. *Well,* I think, *she must be an awfully good singer if she can get away with looking like this.*

When she comes out, wearing chunky white heels and dressed in a loose white silk pantsuit that contrasts with her long black hair, I am not reassured. And when she sings arias by Handel, Rossini, Verdi, and Tchaikovsky, I am not terribly sure she is a good singer. Yet the audience is enthusiastic. Her high range seems harsh and strained; her low range, unnaturally full and mellow. From time to time, I also notice that she drops octaves. Nothing fits. I start to look at my watch and hope that time will fly faster than her trills.

Intermission arrives. We go downstairs for refreshments. At a table Irving converses, in Russian, with a lady. "Curious and curiouser," we want to ask about the singer. By this time, we are wondering whether the soloist is having a bad night or maybe has a bad cold—at one point she cracked and had to leave the stage, coughing.

The woman listens politely to Irving's questions about the singer but annoyingly and frequently corrects his Russian. Every time Irving utters the word for "singer" and uses the feminine ending, the lady across the table promptly alters the word to its masculine form. Irving is tempted to follow the example of Humpty Dumpty and tell the lady, "When *I* use a word, it means just what I choose it to mean. Who is master here?"

Then, of course, the truth dawns. The lady is not remarking on Irving's command of the Russian language but is correcting our misunderstanding. The woman onstage is a man. We have been looking and listening backward. The singer is Erik Salim-Meruet from Russian-Central Asia (Kirghizstan), who was once a choreographer but was discovered ten years ago singing the leading female role in *Madame Butterfly*. Ever since then, he has been a sensation and given concerts all over Central Europe. My friends in Kiev have heard of him.

This general fascination with and acceptance of shifting, uncertain gender boundaries (at least onstage) is what also draws a popular Kiev audience to Boris Moiseev, a gay Russian pop singer, born in jail to a Jewish dissident. In Kiev, after hearing his two most popular songs, "Charlie Parker" and "The Ukrainian Tango" in street cafés, I am curious to see him perform at the Ukrainian Palace.

On the night of Moiseev's concert, crowds stream toward the entrance of the modern theater. I am there, along with three thousand well-heeled, middle-class Ukrainians, who have also brought their children and paid the equivalent of $20 each to watch his two-and-a-half-hour spectacle of bisexuality. Following a crushing crowd, I squeeze past a demonstration outside the theater. I believe the protestors are ultranationalists who object to his being Russian, never mind his homosexuality. I watch the armed militia arrest a few and clumsily shove them into a paddy wagon.

Once past a thick column of security guards as well as a set of metal detectors, I find my seat and wait for the show to start. When it does, Moiseev, earringed and sequined, enters with his "boys." To the pounding and sometimes sugared pulse of his music, he dances (he is trained as a ballet dancer), sings, and ingenuously manipulates his costumed body so that for a period he is female (the pant leg becomes a skirt) and then, with a twist, a male (the skirt reverts to a pant leg). Defying classification, his gender seesaws, rotates, and blends. His body and expression are simultaneously as lyrical as the feathers of a swan and as bullying as a swung thick metal pole. His cropped, slick, bleached hair pulls back to expose a powdered, heavily made-up face. Under the glaring, hot lights, sweat trickles through his features to remind one just how vulnerable life is behind the looking glass.

UNDERGROUND KIEV

Getting there and back is an adventure. As yet, I am not comfortably conversant with the metro system. Alien place names composed in an unfamiliar alphabet, as well as the system's web of linking underground passages, intimidate me. Armed with a well-fingered map, I practice traveling to the venue the day before the concert. Like Alice, I don't wish to travel the wrong way. Moreover, I certainly don't want to be told off by a guard who might complain to all around me, "She ought to know her way to the ticket-office, even if she doesn't know her alphabet."

Each metro stop displays a different theme. Many are elegant. Fine works of art, patterned mosaic tiles, and glistening chandeliers grace these platforms. In contrast, the half-lit, damp gray underground walkways leading to these stylish spaces incongruously reverberate with the buzzing bustle of banality and distraction. The place hums as determinedly and as vigorously as if one had mistakenly disturbed a hornet's nest. Underneath Kiev, makeshift, tattered cells of a secular, commercial life flourish. Bartholomew's Fair returns to life through the crowd of tables, stalls, and booths set up by people eking out a living. Musicians, beggars, flower sellers, cafés, record shops, toothpaste booths, cigarette stalls (it is possible to purchase one cigarette at a time), butchers selling slabs of lard and ox tongues, mongers marketing stale fish, magazine stands, phone stalls, tables displaying home-made cheeses, baked rolls, sweets, and beer venues crowd the channels. In one particular passage, the young people of Kiev hang out and smoke. In another, a small orchestra plays a tango. Near the entrances, farmwomen cradle kittens and puppies in their arms. Swaddled in innocence and not yet sulking like Alice's kitten or irreverently grinning or disappearing like the Cheshire cat, these balls of fur, like skeins of rare virgin wool, are tempting. "Come buy, come buy!" Fearing I shall succumb, I push past.

The most thrilling moments belong to the metro's escalators. Steeper, longer, and faster than any I have been on before or ever will be again, they take people deep down, down under the city to this hidden stratum of life. One steps onto these moving stairs and wonders if one will ever be released from the descent.

I notice the various postures of those riding up and down. Young people sit; some stand backwards; some have their faces buried in a newspaper or a book; others either pass me in the midst of a quarrel or rise embracing each other, as if they have just resolved their differences; some stare into nothingness; others, gesticulating, chase a fleeing word. A crippled man somehow vigorously maneuvers his wheelchair onto the escalator (there are no lifts) and released from immobility for the moment, glides down effortlessly. A young couple clasps a loose pet rat in their arms. People smile approvingly and utter the "aws" of endearment.

Below Kiev, there are religious as well as secular spaces. Centuries ago, monks lived as hermits underneath the Lavra monastery. Today the devout make pilgrimages to these caves.

With a slender, rapidly burning candle, one descends twisting and darkening stone steps, round and round, into a pitch-black passage bordered by coffins in which are wrapped the relics of particular hermits. Small apertures offer obscurely lit views of cells and chapels. Inside, shelves holding bottled skulls, coated in myrrh, catch the sparse light, and tempt the eye. People press by, bend reverently over the coffins, and piously kiss the relics.

Back aboveground and once more in the glow of day, contemporary monks, in flowing black robes, hasten toward the refectory. It is lunchtime. Scurrying to catch up to them, a dwarf in full habit dashes across the courtyard and enters the hall just before the door slams shut. Blown by the gusts of haste, his robes stream after him. Leaving the courtyard and climbing up a bricked hill back to the noise of the streets, one goes by begging women, gypsies, and stray dogs. At the top, chestnut trees are just bursting into leaf.

IN THE LIGHT OF DAY

Like Alice, I often long to get out of so many dark halls or corridors and wander in the light of day. Morning windows are full of promises. Early, before rising in winter, I listen to the sweeping sounds of a woman who spreads sand over the icy sidewalk. She creates a Japanese garden out of her semicircular motions. Then I hear the clanking of the metal poles as people erect their market stalls up and down the street. When I draw back the long, heavy curtains, my attention turns, as it does every morning, to a black-and-white dog leaning up against the window of the third-floor apartment across the street. Adopting the posture of a prying neighbor who regularly appraises the world from her window, the dog carefully considers each pigeon flying by. The sun, when it appears, warms as well as brightens the room with exquisite tints of light. In the late afternoons and evenings, there are other views. Through the window of a second-floor café facing the opera house, I watch a line of tall narrow cedars sway in the breeze and dip in rhythm with the ballet dancers, practicing inside the rehearsal room. Together, their limbs choreograph a sort of pas de deux. Later that night, before drawing the apartment curtains shut, I gaze at the dazzling red lights of the Budapest Club, kitty-corner from us and cling to illusions of reassuring warmth.

In the mornings, I step onto the street and join a mass of humanity treading the pavements and streaming up and down steps. When the gray showers gather, my elbows ache from holding an umbrella and my back aches from sitting in unheated rooms. I walk by lines of older women who, exposed to all sorts of weather, stand from nine in the morning until seven at night selling plucked chickens, eggs, bottles of horseradish, worm-eaten apples, lavender sachets, and black woolen leggings arranged on upside-down wooden crates. In season, they offer walnuts and, for two blissful weeks, baskets of freshly picked strawberries. (I gorge.) Attempting to generate some warmth during the biting-cold months, they shuffle and sway in chorus from one foot to the other. I wonder if they, like Oska's grandmother in *The Tin Drum*, have bricks, heated on wood-charcoal fires, wrapped in newspaper under their skirts to radiate some warmth. After each sale, their swollen hands count the coins. As if transported from Dickens's London, a homeless child glances furtively at their wares. A drunk, dragged by his impatient Airedale terrier, stumbles past.

Farther on, parked on a sidewalk as broad as a road, are tint-glassed limousines and polished Alfa-Romeos that wait indefinitely with their menacing chauffeurs outside expensive restaurants and Mafia bars secured by guards armed with cellular phones and gas guns. Not approving of Irving's less-than-tailored attire, the Dejavu and the Miami twice refuse him admittance.

Pedestrians, beware: the nouveau riche thinks nothing of driving on the sidewalk. Nearby, groups of roaming dogs, having developed a road sense, wait until the green crossing light shines. I pass the occasional person rummaging through rubbish. No refusal here, for just outside the covered Rynak, in the city center, sits a ragged woman gnawing a raw, discarded beef bone.

For all its rough poverty and coarse contrasts, Kiev's beauty is never spent. Corruption, hard lives, crime, and uncertainties do not destroy the visible elegance of another time, which flashes like shook foil to illuminate the city's grandeur. Buildings and structures as well as the lives within them might fall, gall themselves, but their majesty still radiates. Joining the thousands who walk its broad sidewalks, I move with them. At times it is a pleasure to fall into the rhythm of their brisk steps. Past shining white edifices, I find my way up and down hills that look out over the tree-lined Dnieper River, winding through Kiev and navigating the inquisitive eye through a cityscape mapped by monasteries, squares, monuments, offices, universities, museums, galleries, concert halls, boulevards, embassies, palaces, businesses, hotels, parks, apartment buildings, and botanical gardens. Even in the dusk, when one reaches areas trodden and smudged by industry or colored by the gray weariness of areas made desolate by depressing highrise Stalinist architecture, Kiev shines.

Under the guidance of Natalia (the head of foreign languages), who thoughtfully devotes her Saturdays to escorting us to various parts of the city, I visit art galleries and museums, where older women, wrapped in coats, scarves, and worn fur hats, loll against the exhibits and serve as guards. (Their body sweat and bad breath make one hesitate to draw close enough to ask questions.) At Taras Shevchenko University, she takes me to an extraordinary cabinet of curiosities that reminds me of the illustration introducing Ferrante Imperato's 1599 *Dell' Historia Naturale*. It displays stuffed mammals, curious shells, small marine specimens, almost lifelike bird skins, covered jars with brains, diseased organs, or malformed fetuses, arranged horns, tusks, minerals, and boxes of unidentified specimens. Hanging from the ceiling are large fish and even a stuffed crocodile. (*How appropriate,* I think, *that I, who have found myself in a place that is "curiouser and curiouser," should be taken here.*) My life is better for these excursions, and so is my understanding of a city that can be simultaneously beautiful and damaged, pastoral and strident, lasting and vulnerable.

Together we linger before grand homes, such as Gorodetsky House, designed by a nineteenth-century businessman who was passionate about hunting in Africa. Sculpted elephants, tigers, zebras, exotic birds, mermaids, fish, and insects protrude from the corners, doors, windows, and steps of the house and, like gargoyles of empire and authority, gaze down upon the unwitting passersby. We pause while Natalia removes an envelope of paling black-and-white snapshots from her bag so that I might see her (forty or more years ago) as a child, dressed in her buttoned winter coat, standing primly with her parents before the very spot on which we now stand.

She has spent hours going through albums so she can share these with me. I am moved. But why has she done this? Do these images of time past represent a quest for survival or constancy in a life ruled by revolutions, death, and oppressive policies that continuously overturn and try to make nonsense of what one has known or wishes to be? Or are they some futile gesture intended to reclaim a time of innocence and a feeling of being protected? Perhaps these snapshot are also expressions of identity and belonging: these places, defined by the presence of Natalia's revered father, pictured in the snapshot, seem to comprise the scaffolding of her being.

Sometimes Natalia and I meet at 36 Bohdan Khmelnitski, walk up the hill, past the Golden Gate, turn left toward St. Sophia and St. Michael's (in the process of renovation, its gold dome sparkles in the afternoon sun), cast a skeptical glance at the deceptive orderliness emanating from the authoritatively columned exteriors of imposing parliament buildings, and turn to look down over the river, visible to us through spikes of light that dart through openings in the woods. We board a funicular that takes us down among dappled treetops to lower Kiev, where we wander through the peaceful, cloistered grounds of a monastery, stroll by a hat factory, its sewing machines muted for the weekend, and stand outside Kyiv-Mohyla, another large university in the city, where police guards and a busload of militia wait, uncannily silent and at attention, for another attack on the Communist Party headquarters across the road. The day before, radical left-wing demonstrators poured gasoline throughout the building.

Walking back to the funicular, we pause before black ribbons fluttering from Ukrainian flags to commemorate the death (on May 4,1999) of fifty coal miners in the Zasyadko mines, near Donetsk, in the eastern part of the country. These mines are notoriously dangerous, for not only are they unusually deep and produce high levels of methane gas but also they are owned by corrupt politicians who meddle with the hazard-measuring equipment in order to claim that the mine is meeting safety standards. In years to come, three hundred more will fall victim to the black death of the coal mine's blast. In 2015, rescue attempts from yet another disaster at the mine will be hindered by crossfire between Ukrainian government forces and pro-Russian rebels.

Gathering our thoughts, Natalia and I enter a compartment. Inch by inch, the funicular rises above the streets below, brushes by round balls of mistletoe attached to the slope's upper branches, and returns us to the bustle of the upper city.

On another Saturday, we walk through the golden dust of fallen leaves, down a hill, and onto a footbridge that crosses the Dnieper River and leads to a sandy, scruffy island where one can stroll and purchase a drink or a snack. Feeling relaxed in the warming afternoon light, Natalia and I sit at one of the three tables in a café, drink tea, and chat—that is, until a burly, muscular man with slick black hair and the remnants of a broken nose enters with his portable TV, plugs it in, and, after increasing the volume, higher and higher, turns his attention to the boxing match on the screen. Intimidated, annoyed, and momentarily caught in yet another of the brutal contradictions of Kiev, we leave.

Walking through Kiev is a mysterious act, for there is always the unseen and unexpected. Behind the sightless walls of the university's administration building a pleasant park hides in a ravine. Around its uncharted corners, the sweet odors of lilac trees wait for the unsuspecting flaneur. Primroses and violets grow between the tall chestnuts, limes, and birch trees. From a distance, magnolia blossoms glisten like a pond's reflecting surface. On their way to and from work, people find courage in their perfume. In modest restaurants tucked into alleys, caged finches sing while customers sip cups of hot tea; video screens display models parading on fashion-house runways. On back streets, cafés buried in basements vibrate to the sounds of a pulsing techno beat that quickens the blood and, like a shot of espresso, keeps the body in motion. After our time together, Irving and I take Natalia to lunch in these hidden spots. In one the owner hands Irving a cigar on a plate, complete with cigar clipper, and brags in a loud whisper, "Contraband."

Sometimes I prefer to go silently, without Natalia's direction. One quiet, sunny November morning, I walk by a woman who watches contentedly over her demure hen and indecorously plumed rooster while they scratch around under the fir trees planted outside the opera house. She has carried them out of her crowded flat so they can feel and take nourishment from the earth. Nearby a crow hangs on a grapevine crawling up and clutching the side of a building. The bird delicately but greedily picks with his beak the last two grapes of the season.

Farther on, I rest in one of the many Ukrainian churches so as to be among the colorful religious images painted directly onto every centimeter of speechless walls and columns. Devout elderly people kneel before the altar. Their hands, clutched shut, clasp their thoughts. And then I continue down the hill until I reach Kreshatyk, so I might join yet others who have come to seek release from their crowded living quarters and the niggling cares of life.

On weekends, this main, expansive boulevard, stretching for several miles, is closed to traffic. The whole of the city comes out stylishly dressed to promenade and talk with friends, no matter what the weather. As if responding to the deep, quietly running currents of the Dnieper River, people gather in groups and move in gentle waves along the boulevard. Observed at a distance from a second-floor café window, their moving figures resemble hieroglyphic letters spread across an unfurled scroll—a text, or perhaps an illusion, of community. How hard that community is to find now. If only one could superimpose this image over the horror and discord that is to follow in this very spot in 2014.

Loudspeakers lining the streets blast out romantic songs and, for the moment, smooth any disharmony, small or large, that might normally disrupt an afternoon. While promenading down Kreshatyk, those around me give the illusion of stepping away from the confusing linguistic world that can (and will) be divisive and that has the potential to destroy or compromise lives in the years to come. In Kiev, most people speak and read Russian, but public announcements, posters, signs, and university lectures and examinations are, as the government requires, in Ukrainian. The newspapers, however, are in Russian (except for the English-language *Kyiv Post*). Most in Kiev speak a mixture of Ukrainian and Russian or speak one language at home and another at work. In the western part of Ukraine, the Russian language is not welcomed. While I am here, ultranationalists murder a musician in Lviv for singing in Russian. In Crimea, however, Russian is preferred. When Russia reclaims Crimea, it bans Ukrainian, as well as the Tartar language from the schools. Supposedly, a fourteen-year-old boy, discovered speaking the Tartar language on a phone, is beaten on March 31, 2014.

In Odessa I meet an elderly woman, a Ukrainian nationalist, who has vowed never to speak a word of Russian—she forbids it in her house. Tied to the disaster of "nation building," the ammunition of language creates borders and structures its checkpoints. In February 2014, Ukrainian parliament is to ban Russian as the second official language. The vote is later overturned.

On Kreshatyk, I join the pace of these weekend strollers and enjoy what I understand all too well to be the illusion of becoming part of their world. When one does not speak the language, there is something reassuring, even transformative, about falling into the physical rhythm of the people who surround one. A Strauss waltz clatters imperfectly through the static of the loudspeakers and drowns out the bewildering variety of words and tongues that confuse my daily life. The melody's familiar rhythms silence the bits of modern Greek, Spanish, French, Hungarian, and German darting through the humanities building's corridors. Moreover, the waltz's predictable measure regularizes the syncopated mixture of Ukrainian, Russian, German, Latin, Yiddish, and Byelorussian that I heard the previous evening at an event held at the Actor's Guild (formerly a Persian-style Karaite synagogue), and that generally baffles my understanding.

MAIDAN 1999

The section of Kreshatyk that leads to the Maidan, or Independence Square, is the heart of the city. At night, too, this area is often closed to traffic so that people can come together and attend outdoor concerts or rallies. One late evening, after attending an opera, a friend from England and I walk down to

Kreshatyk to join the crush of thousands who have congregated in the square to listen to a rock concert. Images of the band blast out of a huge television screen. Celia turns to me and says, "I wonder what it was like being here ten years ago."

As if on cue, bright blue and yellow beams pulsate and send shafts of Ukrainian light across the gathered multitude. Archival footage of celebrations in Independence Square, on the very day (1991) Ukraine separated from Russia, replaces the televised images of the performing musicians. How ironic that almost fourteen years later, in 2014, over eight hundred thousand people are to rally in the same spot to protest the loss of that promise and register their frustration over closer and closer ties with Russia.

In the Maidan in 1999, Celia and I watch on-screen carefully edited sequences of people fighting for and celebrating their independence. Fireworks burst over our heads. Flaming remnants fall dangerously among us. Dodging rockets, fires, and burning candles, Celia and I, as well as thousands of others, anxiously find our way back along Kreshatyk. Little do they, or we, know that we are benignly enacting what is to be a deadly retreat fourteen years later, when in February, 2014, Independence Square will turn into a battlefield and be the scene of horrific clashes between riot police and thousands of protestors distraught over a repressive, corrupt government that suddenly has turned its back on economic ties with the West.

In 1999, however, Celia and I are merely worried that the falling fireworks might ignite our coats or our hair, so we rush through streets where fifteen years later the police, armed with guns, and snipers will randomly shoot at protestors, who, barely protected by makeshift shields, will run up a nearby hill for safety. A hotel, close to where we pass, will become a makeshift hospital. The wounded will be rushed in, but the medical supplies will be inadequate and many will die from direct shots to their heart, neck, and lungs. It will be the worst day of violence for nearly seventy years. At least eighty-eight will be killed in the space of forty-eight hours.

For the time being, though, Kiev holds its breath. Civil war is a distant, rumbling prospect. For the present, at least, congregating in public is a unifying act. Walking especially is a communal experience, particularly on memorial days. Whatever divisiveness might exist seems to surrender to a shared memory and to give way to the collective rhythms of bodies, moving, moving along streets and boulevards.

WALKING

In March on Women's Day, Kiev becomes a moving garden. Everything shuts down. Through the streets of Kiev, people carry and receive flowers; men (supposedly) cook or take a woman out to dinner, and families meet to stroll and talk together. Main streets, now emptied of moving vehicles, accommodate multitudes of men, women, and children, going to and fro, carrying long-stemmed roses, tulips, or small bunches of lily of the valley and violets.

In a similar mode, later, on May 9, the entire city comes out to honor "heroes" and to pay tribute to those who served in the armed forces. The day begins with a parade of World War II survivors, accompanied by their offspring. Medals pinned to their jackets clang and swing in rhythm with their gait. Afterward, the public walks from monument to monument in order to show their respect and lay flowers at each. Blossoms float in fountains and lie, heaped and fragrant among their stems, on marble steps. Booths selling food, drinks, and small toys edge the street. Millions are walking, walking, walking down and up the hills, by the river, through the parks. After eleven hours on my feet, I reach home.

The following day, people return to Kreshatyk to see an exhibit of mounted, oversize, archival photographs displaying the destruction that the boulevard suffered in the 1940s. Interspersed among these are images of Babi Yar (for the day, consciousness of this event has moved aboveground), concentration camps, and "Ukrainian" military leaders. Memorials have a way of momentarily equalizing loss.

THE SEASONS

Walking is not just for fine, memorialized days; it also part of Kiev's mundane life, in which people diurnally tread and go about their business through the shifting seasons and changing winds. Between February 1, 2000, when I arrive, and my departure, in the middle of December 2000, not only does life fluctuate and reverse itself, but so does the weather, which twists and turns like a petulant child. On foot most of the time, I am acutely sensitive to these forces and variations. The winter I have come to is unusually mild, the warmest since 1895. That, of course, does not mean it is warm. Often, on my way to the university, I feel a damp wind blowing, slicing whatever is in its way. Negotiating slippery hills and skidding on icy streets, I shiver. Irving buys a politically incorrect muskrat hat, and I wear a long, cashmere coat.

In March, spring drizzles start to replace the icy rain. Buds appear. I actually go out without my hat—a good thing because I am tired of it. By April, it's suddenly warm weather. The central committee or central something-or-other has not yet turned off the heat. In search of relief, we fling the windows wide open and let the flies, yellow jackets, and bees peruse our apartment. The radiators steam away; we wilt. I know, however, that the weather will change and cold wind will yet again blow through Kiev. Outside, crews of scarved women and capped men turn over the soil, flattened by frost. They sow grass seed, tidy the edges of flower beds, and transform the disorder of the winter's freezing into the warmth of order and promise—if only their powers to correct the corrupted earth would extend beyond their purview so as to cultivate a more fruitful governing body.

In May, lilies of the valley decorate offices, metro stations, and tabletops. Their perfume is refreshing. The tall, old chestnut trees for which Kiev is famous still hang on to their candle blossoms. Only in the last few days do their petals float through the air and settle, crushed on the pavement. Now the maples soar in their greenness. Toward the end of the month, engineers shut off the water for several days so they can clean the pipes.

In the suns of early autumn, the leaves fall through the smoky light of evening. But in the saturating, dreary rains that follow, this promise of a golden autumn vanishes. Out come the space heater and the hot-water bottles. I even light the oven. Not since childhood have I had to live in an unheated place. Heat will not come on until the end of October. The dampness is debilitating. By November, all the leaves have fallen and now the landscape in the city begins to resemble the way it was when I arrived, last February. Darkness casts broader and heavier shadows over Kiev, so that 5:00 p.m. feels like midnight. In the watery light of day, the trees, brutally pruned of their branches, stand naked like sculpted, limbless torsos, but, as if compensating for their loss, allow uninterrupted views of the city and its architecture.

Throughout the seasons, Natalia and other friends, proud of their national culture, make it possible for me periodically to see other parts of Ukraine. In October we travel, with a hired driver, sixty miles northwest of Kiev to the small town of Pereyaslov (population: thirty thousand), which holds an extraordinary collection of twenty-five museums dedicated to Ukrainian culture. Neither our driver nor we have the slightest idea of how to find or even enter these museums. In Ukraine, there are no pamphlets to guide one.

As instructed, the driver motors slowly through the town's streets to see if he can spot a certain Michael Ivan Sikorski, who might help. Consulting a faded, crinkled photograph of Sikorski, the driver distractedly steers the car, one eye on the road, the other on the imperfect image of Sikorski. Miraculously, before long, the driver spots the guide cum curator, aged, worn, and weighed down by iron keys, ambling slowly down a side street. He agrees to take us around. The problem is that he speaks only Ukrainian (no Russian is spoken in this town). Irving does his best. As far as we can tell, no other visitors are here. People, curious, stare at us.

One museum is the house of Skovorada, an eighteenth-century philosopher (perhaps the Ukrainian equivalent of a Thoreau). In this damp, cold, and barely secured dwelling are ten thousand rare books that belonged to Skovorada and his philosophical school. Many lie in disorderly heaps on desks and tables. Most sit compromised and exposed to the elements, as well as to the indiscriminate fingers of the curious. We gasp as the curator carelessly pulls fifteenth-century texts from open shelves, badly in need of repair. After randomly thumbing through ancient atlases, rare Latin texts, and hand-colored illustrations in eighteenth-century natural-history volumes (one partially nibbled and shredded by a mouse that has made a nest of its exotic ancestors), I anxiously inquire if these books are catalogued. The answer is no; there is no funding. While various groups in Kiev rage over where they should go, these forgotten treasures are being left to rot, like forgotten prisoners, behind a locked door.

We move on to the Museum of Transportation, which houses all shapes and sizes of sledges, once necessary but now obsolete. And then we approach the house of Shalom Alechem, a Yiddish writer of the early twentieth century. When he was alive, 60 percent of Pereyaslov's population was Jewish. Now there are a mere three hundred Jews remaining. As the day continues and we see more of these decaying abandoned places, I feel more and more enveloped by a landscape of loss and deteriorating memory. It is almost a relief to meet our driver so we can go back to the distractions and cosmopolitanism of Kiev.

On the return journey, we pass through the flat agricultural land that once made Ukraine the breadbasket of the world. Occasionally, fields of sunflowers relieve the sight of dried and gnarled leaves about to fall from the trees bordering the darkening road. Like shaken granules of black pepper, swarms of evening crows spread across the sky. Dropped off at 36 Bohdan Khmelnitski, from the backseat of the car, I gather the apples I have taken from a room in yet another museum, the house of Taras Shevchenko (the nineteenth-century poet, serf, painter, and revolutionary after whom the university is named), so that I can spread them out in flat number 8. Like the ones assembled in tumbling throngs on the tables and shelves in Tschvchenko's dining room, they emit a fragrance that will perhaps help prolong a memory of an enlightened, thoughtful past.

There are other brief sojourns. One is to Kamianets-Podilskyi, a historic town in western Ukraine. On a cold, dead early-winter morning, a driver arrives. His well-worn car runs alternately and forever off gasoline and propane—a good thing, too, for the reassuring presence of a lighted petrol station is not to be part of our lonely seven-hour journey. Beyond the outskirts of Kiev, we seem to be the only ones who have ventured onto the roads across a landscape still and coated in ice. Only occasionally does a local truck emerge from the frost and come toward us like a phantom of the nameless in search of identity. Frozen crystals coat every branch, leaf, and blade and, from time to time, catch the sun to weave the coarse countryside into an ethereal fabric. The sheer beauty of it helps ease the fear that the car might skid and bring everything to an end. After interminable hours, the driver pulls over and points to a snack bar, an apparition out of nowhere. With the exception of the owner, it is empty. Desperate not only for hot tea and a sandwich but also for a toilet, I ask where the latter might be. The man behind the bar points to the café's entrance and says, "To the right."

I find an outhouse that once had a door. It borders and faces the road. Shivering, I sit, staring into the iced land and slick highway, relieving myself, on view to any vehicle or person who might venture by. I do not care.

In a few hours, we arrive in the night's darkness and go up to our hotel room. But privacy is to be elusive. No sooner have I swung my overnight case onto the bed than I hear a knock at the door. I open it to find a television crew that wants to come in and interview us. They do. Cameras, interpreter, and interviewer fill up the room. They ask why we are here et cetera. I do my best. The area is starting to promote tourism.

We are here because Kamianets-Podilskyi is a place that has witnessed one bloody power struggle after another. Ever since the thirteenth century, Mongol Tartars, Poles, Russians, Austro-Hungarians, Armenians, Soviets, Germans, and even Ottomans have claimed it. It was briefly the de facto capital of Ukraine. The city has been partitioned, conquered, divided, oppressed, captured, fortressed, and seized. It has seen horrendous massacres, the most recent of which was the mass murder of 23,600 Hungarian and Ukrainian Jews in the space of just two days, August 27, 28, 1941. Starting in the eleventh century, different peoples and cultures have brought their own culture and architecture to the area. Each has left evidence of its secular and religious life. In the frozen haze, ghosts of old monasteries, churches, cathedrals, schools, town halls, synagogues, Turkish minarets, market squares, and houses congregate like lost and damaged souls among the rubble and cobbled streets of the Old Town. Two hundred buildings, some intact and some in ruins, from the eleventh to the nineteenth centuries, populate the area. The Smotrych River swirls in a deep canyon to create an island that isolates these remains from the central part of the city (a fortressed bridge connects the two). Its rushing waters and dramatic rocks segregate the remembrance of what was once a vibrant, multiethnic, theological-philosophical, though by no means always harmonious, community from its monocultural, industrial, unaesthetic present. The silent, secluded, unpopulated island is a graveyard.

On the last day, while I walk the streets of the Old Town, my attention wanders to a door, just ajar enough that I can see inside. A group of very young, obedient boys, paintbrushes in hand, bend conscientiously over slabs of wood and pots of paint. An elderly monk instructs them. The boys are learning, from scratch, to design and paint icons. One embodied phantom of the past, at least, haunts the ruins.

CHAPTER 6:

In Ruins Laid

ODESSA AND CRIMEA

Odessa

In April, when spring warms the earth, Natalia arranges for me to go down to the State University of Odessa to offer a series of classes on contemporary American multiculturalism—a generous gesture on the part of the university's Department of Foreign Literature. Because there are no available texts, I bring

Xeroxed copies of the literary selections I shall be discussing. The students take notes quietly and attentively. They wait until after each class to ask me questions.

While in Odessa, I am also asked to talk about recent trends in American literature to graduate students and professors from Ukraine and, interestingly, also from Russia. (In Odessa, the Russian connection is stronger than it is in Kiev.) Panicked and not sure what to do, I prepare a paper on the electronic poetry I have seen demonstrated at Brown University, as well as in workshops at the University of Buffalo. Though I have no means of showing examples (computers are just not part of this space), I try verbally to illustrate what these works would look like on a computer screen and speculate as well on how these poems not only upset the traditionally static linear form of poetry but also dismiss the single figure of the poet. Rather than standing still on the page, these digitized poems respond to computer programs that allow interactive readers randomly and continuously to rearrange the poems' words, syllables, and lines. On the screen, the text becomes tentative and fluid. To complicate matters, most of the audience is not conversant in English, so I must speak via an interpreter, an experience that I find disorienting, for it slices thought into slim phrases and unnaturally introduces caesura into the running rhythms of consciousness.

Like many occasions, the event makes me anxious, for it places me too much in the position of being an "expert." Throughout my time in Ukraine, one problem for me is that people assume I know anything and everything about American literature. And, of course, I don't. If I am unsure about a particular fact or work, I feel as if I am letting down not only them but also myself. And then I am frustrated because the library holdings are weak; it is more often than not impossible to fill in blanks or dig more deeply into critical responses to a writer. This circumstance increases my admiration for most of my colleagues, who have never been to America or taken many courses in its literature but know more than I. Their commitment to learning, to absorb as much as they can, and incessantly read all they can get their hands on, is incredible.

In truth, by sending me to Odessa, Natalia is not just putting me to work but also granting me (and Irving) a holiday. She has also allowed me eight days off from teaching to be a "tourist." Even though we are pleased to be going and are packed, the thought of uprooting ourselves from Kiev, making sure that we have the right documents and enough cash feels troublesome. I also dread the fifteen-hour, overnight train journey. I have grown dependent on what has become familiar to me in Kiev, as well as on Natalia's supervision.

At the train station, I am reminded yet again of my colleagues' selfless generosity. Three have come to see Irving and me off. Like anxious parents, they huddle together on the platform and press their faces up to the windows to make sure we are seated in the correct compartment and that we have brought food and water—no refreshments are available on the train. As they shut the compartment door, they reassure us that people from Odessa will be at the station to meet us. It is awful to admit that at the same time I am moved, as well as reassured, by their attention, part of me looks forward to be going to a place where I am, for a while, to be left to myself.

Once, Odessa was a splendid city with Eisenstein's Potemkin Steps going down to a harbor, vibrant with bustling naval and military commerce, not to mention the illicit trade of the Mafia. In 2000, it is a city in crisis where buildings are, with a few exceptions, left to crumble; where weeds suffocate once meticulously manicured parks; where projects started ten years ago are abandoned; and where the palaces of the rich stand deserted and lonely. Throughout the city, cracks and smashed windows compromise grand architectural structures. When I walk through the center, it is hard to imagine that fourteen years later, the place will be at war with itself and that on May 2, 2014, forty-two pro-Russian activists will die, trapped in the burning Trade Union Building close to where I stand.

No tourists come to Odessa in 1999 or early 2000. About ten years ago, there were many visitors from not only Eastern but also Western Europe. We ask why. One answer is that people stopped coming after the fall of the Soviet Union. Pollution is not as regulated as it was during Soviet rule, so now the effluents from the factories and spillage from the sewers get trapped in the circular currents of the Black Sea and cause a "big stink." Some people, at least those with means, have other choices, so they go where they believe the waters are cleaner. Those who cannot move are subjected to the contaminating uncertainties of the present and condemned to a place that is disintegrating around them. No wonder some of the older generation long for another time, whether good or bad, when certainty and predictability seemed to attend Soviet rule.

For all this, however, in the 1990s Odessa is still a center of culture, though a fading and struggling one. Phantoms of Babel (his house is there) and a young Horowitz (the music academy and concert hall remain) waft in and out of consciousness. At a literary museum, a dogged curator surreptitiously introduces controversial exhibits by hanging items behind doors or up high so that when officials come they don't notice these censored documents. Two art galleries and a dusty archaeological museum continue. And so does the Jewish Library, where, behind a basement door, I discover a small, lighted classroom packed full of young Orthodox Jewish boys, each with a chessboard in front of him. Concentrating over their game, they sit in silent, attentive rows. It is an image to remember.

After we leave the train, my first task is to get in touch with the dean of the university in order to know when and where I am to lecture. I am to call her at the prearranged hour of 3:00 p.m. Arriving several hours before then, we decide to eat lunch

in the Londonskaya Hotel, the one remaining fashionable hotel in Odessa, situated at the head of the Potemkin Steps. The hotel is a nineteenth-century gothic wonder.

We enter an ornate dining room and find ourselves utterly alone. During the meal, we suffer through obsequious service. If I move my spoon, the waiter immediately runs to the table and straightens it. We also suffer from eating an oily salad. Later, I joke that it must have been made of surplus ship oil. The result is that in the hotel lobby, from which Irving makes the preliminary call to the dean (I need him to speak Russian to the secretary), he is overcome with an urgency for the toilet, but he cannot get off the phone because this is my only chance to find out what I am supposed to do. While waiting for the dean to get on the line, he squirms and turns to me, saying, "I can't make it. Ann, you'll have to manage—and where's the toilet?" Irving throws the phone over to me and rushes down the hall, but as soon as the dean begins talking, the salad oil also turns on me. Thankfully, the conversation is short; then, I, too, shoot down the hall. We emerge, laugh, and recover sitting at the head of the steps, which are disappointingly less dramatic than I hoped they might be.

ARCADIA

The State University of Odessa has arranged for us to stay a few miles from the city in a sanatorium hotel, the Magnolia, near the sea and just a ten-minute walk from the university—for which I am grateful since one of my lectures is eight in the morning. At that lecture, I discover a swastika chalked on the blackboard. It is erased at my request.

In spite of this sobering reminder of indelible prejudice, it feels good to be away from the dark, crowded passages of Kiev and out in the open light of the ocean and its skies. From our sparse room, it is possible to look out to sea and cast the eye toward a grassy path that follows the coast and takes the walker eight miles to the center of Odessa. Sometimes, as is the practice, we hitch rides.

Later, I amble along this way, past eight grazing goats and a herder, who, involved in reading his book, commands his dog to keep the animals in order. The goats pay no heed and repeatedly butt the poor animal, who must do his duty until his master lifts his eyes from the page and once more takes control. A few yards along, two middle-aged "spinsters" lovingly carry their two pet crows in matching wicker baskets. The ladies talk incessantly to their birds but not to each other. It is the Orthodox Easter weekend, so in the sun of midday the whole of Odessa picnics by the sea. Holidaymakers and dogs peer through gaps among the tall, breezing grasses. Sounds of people sawing branches off trees and of children picking up twigs announce the building of fires. Family and friends cluster around barbecues. Greased bodybuilders flex their muscles before critical and sometimes indifferent eyes. Along the promenades and down on the beaches, children gladly display their nascent acrobatic, karate, and boxing skills.

Eventually, snatches of amplified Ukrainian poetry and song drift irregularly toward shore from a platform stretching into the sea. It is time to return. In the early evening, a hedgehog modestly yet deliberately makes its quiet way through the grasses; on a bare branch above him, a species of woodpecker I have never seen before rocks back and forth in search of insects.

We are staying in an area called Arcadia, a region devoted to sanatoria designed to assuage all manner of troubles and diseases. There are clinics for the digestion, the liver, the eyes, and for alcoholism—paradoxically, this clinic stands next door to a champagne distillery. Enough remains of these grand buildings for one to understand that Arcadia was once utterly blissful, a place of rest for those who were wealthy and luxuriated in their problems. These magnificent places now stand either empty or slightly modernized (but not to a Westerner's eye).

Some sanatoria have been adapted to house patients supported by state funds and a few maintained to accommodate private patients. All the land around them is unkempt and overgrown. When I ramble alone, uninvited, through the grounds of these relics of another time, I watch attendants in white uniforms officiously walk from building to building through tall weeds, past dry fountains, over structurally unsound stone bridges, and then stride by damaged sculptures of discus throwers and Cossack maidens sheltered by old lime, maple, and chestnut trees. Stray dogs live in grottos next to glass conservatories overtaken and burst asunder by the plants, which have grown through and up the sides of these structures. In between stand half-finished modern buildings (abandoned for lack of funds) and all the mess that accompanies incompleteness. Along the paths metal spikes, treacherous holes, and rotten steps lead down to the sea and discarded dreams.

At the Magnolia, we have full room and board for $20 per day. All the meals are essentially the same. Breakfast consists of gruel, radishes, green onions, sardines, meatballs, kasha, dry bread, and tea with heaping spoonfuls of sugar. Lunch offers soup, dry bread, cabbages, radishes, meatballs, potatoes, and stewed plums. Dinner is composed of radishes, sardines, meatballs, kasha, a roll, and (finally) butter. Thankfully, I am spared the grubby "healing" glasses of water served to Ukrainian guests, who have come for their health and after meals recline in grungy-looking mud baths leftover from a previous century or loll in the healing waters piped from some nearby spring into decaying mineral baths. The stray cats and dogs benefit from the meatballs I don't always eat. Ladies wearing frilly aprons speak in diminutives and cast kind but disapproving matronly looks if I leave anything on my plate. Under the long plain wooden table, an orange kitten slides on the linoleum floor and attacks trouser legs. Occupants who obediently eat everything cast curious but polite looks in our direction. We nod back.

Two men assigned to the dining table next to us move toward us. "May we have the teapot?" evolves into a halting conversation in Russian with Irving. Eventually, they ask if we would like to visit a monastery. Ready for anything, though clueless about where and what order it is, we agree.

At eight that evening (rather late, we think), we climb into their small but well-equipped vehicle. After winding through main streets and alleys for half an hour, and after they stop to buy bottles of liquor, we find ourselves on the grounds of a monastery we can barely see. Abruptly leaving us in the car, the two jump out and obsequiously embrace the monks strolling in the courtyard. After returning to the car, they drive on farther, to where there is a small outer building, which is the dwelling of the most revered of the order. Outside stand long, quiet, shadowed lines of deferential men and women waiting for hours to be blessed. Whenever the door opens and momentarily extends a ray of light, each supplicant excitedly peers over the shoulder of another worshipper to try and catch a fleeting glimpse of his divine presence.

Increasingly puzzled in the backseat, we watch as our "friends" extract the purchased bottles of liquor from the car's boot, break through the rows of patient, devout believers, and like a two-headed Hydra, slither effortlessly and rapidly into the divine's quarters. The door slams behind them. More than curious and a bit impatient, I cautiously get out of the car and peer through a small windowpane proffering a view of the interior. It is a scene out of *The Decameron*: the divine monk and our two acquaintances are lustily imbibing the purchased liquor, glass after glass. With their feet up on the desk, they laugh raucously and slap their thighs. When a lady attendant catches sight of me, she jumps up and immediately draws the curtains to block my view. I return to the car.

After an interminable time, our two companions reappear; the monk follows them out. Oblivious to what has taken place inside, the followers, who have been patiently waiting for an audience, raise their voices in ecstatic religious song and bow down low before the sight of the holy monk.

This is only the beginning. Our drivers inform us that a friend of theirs (a monk) needs a ride to another monastery. We wait silently in the car. After a number of uncomfortable minutes, to our surprise, both a monk and a nun appear. How are we all to fit in? There are now six of us. I am moved to the front seat, but Irving is relegated to the back, where he sits pressed between one man and a portly monk. The nun, in full habit, places herself on Irving's lap. The ride to the other monastery is wild and reckless. The men stop for yet more liquor. Maneuvering treacherously through alleys and swerving around potholes, gullies, and trenches, the car bounces in the sinister darkness, through a long-deserted military barracks, where it almost crashes into a wrecked, discarded airplane before entering a flooded courtyard that looks more like a lake than like solid ground. Ignoring my complaints as well as the nun's Ave Marias, the driver plows through, scrapes the bottom of the car, and stops suddenly still. In this pitch-black, lonely, gaping yard of a monastery, everything unexpectedly becomes ethereal and dreamlike.

I am not prepared for what happens next. Like a floating apparition, a single Ukrainian Orthodox priest—bearded, tall, and in full regalia—suddenly emerges from the unpeopled darkness into the form-giving brightness of the car's headlights. In measured, hushed, ritual steps, he slowly approaches us. High above his head, he holds the order's most sacred icon. The car's beams catch the sheen of its golden ornamentation. Astonished, we fall quiet and stare. While he and the icon drift silently by before rejoining and disappearing into the black of night, the nun on Irving's lap, overjoyed in the presence of this holy relic, rapturously cries out, "Christ be with you" time and time again. That night it is a relief to return to the Magnolia.

As if needing to return to the underground spaces that are so much a part of our life in Kiev, before leaving Odessa we hire a driver (in a Mercedes—the wife comes along, too) and an English-speaking guide to take us to the catacombs, a series of submerged caves dug into the sides of intricately webbed underground passages, in a village just outside of Odessa. It was in these catacombs that the partisans in World War II hid and conducted their covert operations. Walking through two miles of subterranean walkways, constructed on two levels, we see where these courageous individuals had, in spite of mammoth hardships, slept, cooked, washed, and tapped sources of water.

After the tour, we climb back into the Mercedes and bump along ditches to the house of the driver's mother. The driver used to be a chef in the army. He cooks lunch while his dog, knowing he is not allowed in, sulks in the doorway. Next we go to the English guide's flat in the city, where we must listen, for hours, to her daughter's boyfriend play the piano. We have a hard time getting away.

It is time to leave Odessa. I wait outside the Magnolia on a patio that overlooks a run-down swimming pool, a clinic, and a tacky sculpture depicting a young boy and girl facing each other with adoring looks. When the person from the university arrives to take us to the train, she points to this sculpture and, in her imperfect English, asks me what I think of it. I am about to proffer my opinion, when, fortunately, she interrupts me to say that it is of her daughter and son-in-law. Saved.

Before we board the train and endure a sleepless, overnight ride back to Kiev (I seem to have bronchitis), our kind faculty escort, attempting to show off her English, pops her head into the compartment and with the best of intentions bids me a hearty "good riddance!" I know she means to say "good-bye" or something like that, but, once uttered, whether correct or not, the words grate and make me wonder if perhaps there was no error at all. Such is the faulty nature or truth of language.

CRIMEA

"Oh, thankless Crimean land! In ruin laid /
Are now the castles that were once your pride."
—Mickiewicz.

My department chair, Natalia, is eager for me to see as much of Ukraine as possible, so in October 2000 she insists that I take time off from my lecturing and travel to Crimea. "You cannot be in Ukraine without visiting the area—so beautiful and so restful." Memories of that visit to Crimea beg to be recorded. What was possible then is no longer.

In midmorning, Irving and I board a train for what is going to be an eighteen-hour ride from Kiev to Simferopol, a journey that will become even longer because of an additional four-hour bus ride to Yalta. A uniformed attendant delivers cups of hot tea with lemon and sugar. This tea goes well with the sandwiches I have packed. Waiting for the long night ahead, I look out of the train window. After a week of dreary rains, it is refreshing to see the sparkling sun light up the dewed fields ripe with marrows, pumpkins, beets, sunflowers, and red stubble. It is a season of mellow fruitfulness.

As the train plods by, the window frames a Constable

painting in which a horse attached to a wooden wagon pauses in a stream. Close by domestic geese sway in chorus. A cat sleeps among the zucchini. With her back to the passing train, a woman sits resignedly watching the cows graze from right to left. (I wonder what she thinks about.) As if she belongs to Keats's ode to the season, she watches, with patient looks, hour by hour, the last oozings of autumn. A man riding his bike, loaded with mature acorn squash lashed to its rack, pedals silently through my frame of vision.

As the afternoon lengthens into evening, long shadows start their trespass through slopes of wheat fields. Their shade will soon subdue the rows of cabbages that, in the late light, resemble turtles lined up on a log to catch the healing warmth of the sun's last rays. Like a moving-picture gallery, the train window makes visible Monet's studies of haystacks that capture changes in their aspect and color between dawn and night.

When darkness descends, I pull the blinds, put on the light, open Ralph Ellison's *Invisible Man*, and then buy a newspaper from a man who knows a little English. I learn that he was once a physicist and a headmaster of a school but lost his job after Perestroika. Now, in his worn uniform, he travels the trains selling newspapers. His eye catches sight of my reading. He tells me he has read George Orwell's *Invisible Man*.

That night in my bunk, thinking I hear an intruder (it is really Irving opening the door so he can go to the toilet), I sit up screaming. When Russia invades Crimea in 2014, the train I am on will stop running altogether. The border will be closed tight.

As if I were a worker during that Soviet period, I have been sent for ten days to Crimea for rest and restoration. In 1920, Lenin declared the Crimea the place "for the medical treatment of the Working People." But I am not to go to one of the 138 sanatoria (one for each profession: teachers, doctors, engineers, postal workers, customs officials—even one for actors), where I would be taking three large meals a day, subjecting my body to a complete medical examination, and lowering my blood pressure with the assistance of massages, herbal remedies, and bathing. Neither will I be learning to breathe though the nostrils or the mouth via some medieval-looking contraption that cleans out the lungs, nor enduring the shocks from an electric apparatus in order to restore my balance. And I certainly will not be electing to have leeches applied to my ears so as to improve my hearing. Instead, I am to stay at an Intourist hotel in Yalta—out of season, during a silent, dark, and empty October.

We decide against the one Natalia has booked, for there is no heat and no hot water. After hearing the continuous running of the toilet, noticing the one dangling lightbulb in our room, and eating leathery dumplings served by a pleasant woman with two surly daughters in a drafty bar, we look for another place. The search introduces us to Yalta, for it leads us from hotel to hotel, private apartment to private apartment, by vine-laden cottages bursting with ripe grapes, and along an old-fashioned seaside promenade, where the surf bursts into spray over the walls and scatters unsuspecting pedestrians who, like startled birds, flit in gatherings out of reach. The places are either too small or too expensive, too dark, up ten flights of stairs, or lacking a view of the sea.

As a last resort, we climb a hill to the Hotel Yalta. Friends in Kiev have led us to believe it will not be suitable for our taste, but it is and we move in. Our room is modern, with a balcony overlooking the cream, green, and blue bay of Yalta. The window frames a pristine view of the Crimean mountains. In the mornings, Irving watches the gray clouds move from behind these mountains and drift out to sea.

The Hotel Yalta is monstrous, like some breached, enormous cruise ship. It has 2,300 rooms. Each of the floors has a different character and management. Our floor is run by Intourist and costs $30 per night. Inside are at least five privately owned restaurants, two state-owned restaurants, a post office, a bank,

a money exchange, a tourist bureau, shops, a gym, a swimming pool, a casino, a shoe-repair booth, a twenty-four-hour nurse, and slot machines. When it opened in 1973, the hotel employed more than two thousand people and accommodated the rush of tourists during the postwar years from Russia, its neighboring countries, and Germany. It also thrived on cruises originating in Greece and Turkey. (After Russia reclaims Crimea in 2014, tourism drops severely as the region becomes out of bounds for Ukrainians.)

Out of season, the hotel is cavernous and eerie. On the first evening, we sit alone and dwarfed in a vast, unlit restaurant that seats over six hundred people. As if situated in the bowels of some shipwrecked, rolling ocean liner, the restaurant seems to sway in the shadows cast by candles placed on each of the several hundred tables. Adrift at breakfast on the sixteenth floor, we eat in an equally large restaurant, which looks out on all sides at a vast sea disturbed only by its shuddering, dark swells. Eight waiters serve us.

Irving feels unwell and wishes to rest in bed, so I arrange for a driver in a black Mercedes to pick me up early in the morning, tour the area, and return in the autumn evening. On the first day, we travel more than sixty miles, three-quarters of the way up the Crimean limestone mountains. Following the coast, the car winds its way over forested ravines and through exposed hills and small mountain villages to Sebastopol. This is a city like no other, for it accommodates the naval headquarters of both Ukraine and Russia. (The better-equipped Russian sailors live in their own quarters and get paid more than their Ukrainian counterparts.) For the moment, separate and mixed loyalties roam its streets but do not yet indulge the terrible discord to come. (In the early 1990s, the Russian president, Boris Yeltsin, and Ukraine's Leonid Kravchuk agreed to divide the former Soviet Black Sea Fleet between Russia and the newly formed Ukrainian navy.)

Five years earlier, I would have been refused admittance into this armed city on the Black Sea. Now a roadside checkpoint stands vacant and neglected. Even when it was manned, I am told, people regularly bypassed this barrier by walking through the forest. But this alternative is a short-lived reality. It will not be long before such exits and entrances are sealed and the Ukrainian navy is forced to leave. There will be talk of making Sebastopol an exclusively Russian military city to which no unauthorized people can go. Unidentified gunmen will take over the airport (February 28, 2014), the Russian flag will fly over several official buildings, and Vladimir Putin will sign a bill to absorb Crimea into the Russian Federation.

When I reach Sebastopol, the long coil of war inevitably commands my attention. Sebastopol has seen some of the bloodiest battles and at times has been entirely destroyed. For instance, the Nazis captured the city on July 4, 1942. After World War II, the Russians felt compelled to rebuild Sebastopol stone by stone. The guide and I, feeling it unwise to linger, drive at a deliberate pace past buildings destroyed in both the Crimean War and the Second World War. We make our way along boulevards bordered by various naval industrial sites, isolated and secured behind barbed-fences, until we reach a relic from the past: a nineteenth-century panorama displaying the 1855 siege of Sebastopol. Excited actually to be entering what I have only seen pictured in Victorian publications, I eagerly get out, pay my money, and, translator in tow, dash up the steps to its entrance.

From an elevated circular platform, I look down into a three-dimensional display of the battle, the ships, the canons, the horses, and the fallen men. I read every explanatory plaque. A nineteenth-century engraving published in an 1855 issue of the *Illustrated London News* comes to life before my eyes. I have a hard time believing that I am at the very spot where Russia and combined British, French, and Ottoman forces vied for territory. As if stepping back in time and becoming Fanny Duberly, the wife of the paymaster for the English troops, I mount a hill to become a spectator at the theater of battle so I might watch the smoking, blazing city and listen to guns and musketry. I look down on the heap of ruins and see the transport carts covered in tarpaulins and carrying the dead. I see stacks of piled-up bodies in every stage of putrid decomposition, flung out into the street. But I do not smell the intolerable stench of death. In her diary entry for September 1855, Duberly writes:

> *I think the impression made upon me by the sight of that foul heap of green and black, glazed and shriveled flesh I never shall be able to throw entirely away. To think that each individual portion of that corruption was once perhaps the life and world of some loving woman's heart—that human living hands had touched, and living lips had pressed with clinging and tenderest affection, forms which in a week could become, oh, so loathsome so putrescent!*
> —Mrs. Duberly's War

Back in the Mercedes, the journey continues. Time and place shift. Just outside of Sebastopol, tucked into a corner of industrial and military waste, are the remains of an ancient Greek city, Chersonesus (424 BC). The ruins go right down to the sea and, like picked, bleached bones, stretch out under the glimmering sun. "The Greeks set shining, columned marble here." Time has strewn these ancient columns over a heath that, along with its grasses and wildflowers, does battle with its compromised surroundings.

The guide and I follow a path of cedars, pines, and old oak trees until we are alone with a wind that whips the sky. We stand next to a Greek temple, later transformed into a Christian basilica and turn to look at the clouds racing over a field of sedentary ruins. Suddenly, into the corner of my vision steps a statuesque, young Ukrainian archaeologist, wearing glistening emerald green stiletto heels, who makes her way easily, like some goddess from an ancient pantheon, over shards of remains. As she draws near, her elegant shoes spike the exposed mosaics. The earth that once witnessed long-oared fleets approach its shores accepts her presence. In the far distance, when the sun shines, bathers, like sirens, lie listlessly on adjoining rocks. In the fifth century, as first among a series of invaders and conquerors, the Greeks established colonies along this coast. There is a significant Greek population still in Crimea, even though in June, 1944, the Soviets deported the Greek community, along with Armenians and Bulgarians, as part of an ethnic-cleansing campaign, intent on destroying vestiges of Greek culture. In the 1970s, there are still groups speaking Medieval Greek.

Later, these phantoms of ancient Greece draw me to Balaklava, a long, narrow inlet that for centuries has offered ships protection from the ocean's heaving waves. On one side, a slender street follows this passage to and from the sea. Rows of poplar trees shake like a death rattle in the strong wind and preface a sequence of yellowing, crumbling turn-of-the-century buildings. Above are the remnants of an Italian castle and the foundations of a fourteenth-century church. On the other side are the few remaining husks of nineteenth-century fashionable dachas. Below them, in the harbor, drift the rusted ruins of the Ukrainian navy: like a long-dead walrus, one blackened submarine washes up against the harbor wall. On either side rise steep mountains that stare down upon the harbor. For the moment I share Odysseus's eyes:

> We entered a fine harbor there, all walled around
> by a great unbroken sweep of sky-scraping cliff
> and two steep headlands, fronting each other, close
> around the mouth so the passage in is cramped.
> Here the rest of my rolling squadron steered,
> Right into the gaping cove and moored tightly,
> prow by prow. Never a swell there, big or small;
> a milk-white calm spreads all around the place.
> —Book X, The Odyssey.

It is easy to imagine Odysseus suddenly looking up and seeing "hundreds, not like men, like Giants," hurling stones upon his ships from the mountains above.

> Down from the cliffs they flung great rocks a man
> could hardly hoist
> and a ghastly shattering din rose up from all the ships—
> men in their death-cries, hulls smashed to splinters—
> They speared the crews like fish
> and whisked them home to make their grisly meal.
> "Put your back in the oars . . . now row or die!"
> In terror of death they rippèd the swells.

Death is no stranger to Balaklava, for it was here that the British packed in their war fleets and brought in many of their wounded during the Crimean War.

Roger Fenton's photographs, taken and developed while he traveled in his specially equipped van, not only reveal how dangerously crowded the harbor was but also show images of the nearby exposed hills and valleys looming above this narrow harbor. Spent cannonballs, naval officers, and tent encampments once spread over these plains.

Balaklava catches the imagination, so, when Irving is better and can join me, we return. This time the wind has died down and the sun sees no cloud. We stop for tea at a café under one of the poplar trees. What some might call the village idiot latches on to us and won't let go. He offers to show Irving the way to a public toilet, as there is none in the café. The two leave; Irving returns with stories of the world's filthiest toilet. The cholera that spread through the troops during the Crimean War seems not that far away.

Eventually, a woman at a nearby table rescues us by showing us where we might hire a man to take us in his rowboat to view the harbor. Alone on the water, with our man, we row first to the harbor's entrance, to where the narrow inlet offers passage from the open sea, then to a point from which one can gaze, astonished, at the wild waves dashing against rugged rocks and "sky-scraping cliffs." The boatman then furtively offers to take us into caves burrowed deep into the harbor's surrounding cliffs. Once at their entrance, we duck to avoid becoming entangled in loose strands of barbed wire that once secured these spots from prying eyes. Gliding carefully under sharp, ripping barbs and past skull-and-crossbones signs warning of electric shock and danger, we enter a version of the mouth of hell. Guided by a handheld flashlight, the rowboat moves into a deadly large, dripping, molding interior where the Russians, until 1991, hid their nuclear- submarine fleet from the West's gaze. All is silent except for the occasional splash of the oars. We are in a labyrinth of unfathomable channels under the very ground on which the British troops camped during the mid-nineteenth century. My attention turns to the empty, rusted walkways at the sides of these deep, vaulted caverns; I wonder what feet once trod there and what sounds reverberated through these hidden passages of war. It is almost a relief when the boatman calls a halt to our explorations and pulls his oars back into the sun.

On the way back to Yalta, the car passes acres of vineyards where women stand by the road, selling sixteen varieties of grapes as well as dried fish, which like last week's washing, hang on lines strung from tree to tree. In twos and threes, people walk into the forests to collect mushrooms; workers holding buckets spilling with grapes (payment for their labor on collective farms) wait for local buses. Evening light replaces the brightness of the day's sun. We take a route thousands of feet above the sea so we can look down upon Gorbachev's dacha, a large, heavily secured white estate, where the Soviet leader went in times of trouble and where his phone line was cut during one of the periods preceding his downfall.

Approaching the Baidarsky Pass, the Mercedes climbs higher and higher, out to the edge of a narrow rock protruding from a cliff that plunges steeply into the surf below. Here perches the Foros Church, four hundred meters above the village of the same name. A Moscow tea trader built this Orthodox church to celebrate Alexander's III's survival in an 1888 train disaster. As if replicating the event, the church's traditional Byzantine domes rise defiantly above the structure's dizzying resting place. This structure, too, is a survivor. It too has outlived the violent wreck of history. In 1921, when Crimea became part of the Soviet Socialist Republic and then subject to Stalin's repressions, officials brutally shut down Foros Church. They exiled its priests to Siberia (to death), and destroyed its frescoes by uncaringly splashing white paint over the paintings' brilliant designs and images. Shattered and looking as if it had toppled off its mountain ledge, what remained was eventually transformed into a snack bar for tourists.

The destruction continues. After 1969, the café was closed and the shell of the church sat empty and sacked until the 1980s, when Leonid Kuchma initiated a series of campaigns to finance its restoration. Now, in 2000, alone on the cliff's edge, I gaze at the church as it once was. Its reclaimed white shape, like a paper cutout exhibited on a dark screen, appears before me as an apparition. At its back, the boundless ocean swirls, the night sweeps down from the sky, and gale winds howl. I zip up my leather jacket and tie my scarf more tightly around my neck. Through an open door, the wind whistles and whips down the church's aisles to compete with the solemn, low-pitched, close harmony of the Orthodox priests conducting evening service. Icons and the repaired frescoes, flickering in and out of shadows cast by candlelight, add their voices, too. The priests, the sea, the crags in the darkening night all assemble to remind me that one among them who had raised money for the church's restoration was recently murdered by robbers. Destruction begins again. I wonder now what has happened. Will the whirling gyre of history once more blow its doors shut, exile its priests, and leave the building abandoned?

Another long excursion takes Irving and me through steep valleys between hills of limestone carved out by the wind, along winding back roads, and over mountain passes to the interior of Crimea, to what was once in the fifteenth century the political and cultural center of the Crimean Tatars. We have come to Bakhchysarai, which surrounds us with a mélange of history, conflict, culture, and exile. This central town, now less developed, is a place where live not only Russians and Ukrainians but also Jews, Greeks, Germans, Armenians, Bulgarians, and, most of all, Crimean Tatars. Its architecture helps tell the story of its multiple identities.

We first visit the Khan Palace, built initially in the sixteenth century and used subsequently by a succession of Crimean khans, vassals of the Ottoman Empire, who once controlled Crimea's coastal areas in the fifteenth to eighteenth centuries, until 1783, when the Russian Empire annexed the region. The palace is a combination of Ottoman, Persian, and Italian architecture. Minarets tower above its walls. Inside are a mosque, built in 1532, a harem, lush gardens, a cemetery, and the khan's living quarters, with a private mosque, tiled floors, carved ceilings, and a "fountain of tears," commissioned by one of the khans to commemorate the death of a young Polish concubine. It was made famous by Pushkin's 1822 "The Fountain of Bakhchysarai" and by Adam Mickiewicz's *Crimean Sonnets*. Replicating the khan's grief, the water drops almost silently from one lotus leaf to another, as if a single tear were falling.

As we leave the palace, the sound of prayers coming from nearby mosques drifts along the dusty streets where descendents of the exiled original Tatars sell deep-fried, honeyed pastries swarming with hundreds of wasps. The muezzin voices vibrating through the town tempt one to imagine camel caravans and traders from Turkey gathering in the square.

We proceed up a long hill to a walkway overlooking a narrow river valley and come to yet another steep hill that eventually veers to the right, where we continue our ascent on a rocky path beyond the tree line until we reach two thousand feet. The view into the sharply deep fissures and plunge of the river valley is dramatic. One imagines letting go the grip of time and hurling oneself into the abyss.

We come up to a medieval fortress and the remains of a walled, abandoned community—its dwellings and compartments carved into the mountain limestone—that was home to the Crimean Karaites until the midnineteenth century. Some call it the Jewish Fortress. Because of anti-Semitism elsewhere, these people settled here from the fourteenth century on, especially in the seventeenth and eighteenth centuries. I am reminded of the fact that, from 1923 to 1944, there were efforts to create Jewish settlements in Crimea; concurrently, the Nazis targeted Crimean Jews by recruiting rural Tatar volunteers to search out and murder them.

The rugged stone remains and husks of synagogues (*kenesa*) testify to a former animated Jewish presence. Hebrew inscriptions from the eighteenth century are still visible, as are burial mounds. It is eerie to walk, sometimes crawl, among these ruins in these deserted, windblown places and think they once teemed with life. Ruts of carriage wheels, as in Pompeii, remain in the rock of roads as silent traces of another time. In the midst of this community are also reminders of a powerful Muslim presence. As I search for the path to take us down, I pass by the delicately carved stone mausoleum protecting the grave of a sixteenth-century khan's daughter. Remains of beliefs and peoples tumble together in the wind.

Fascinated, enchanted, we stay up here as long as it is safe. We descend into the sinking sun, walk past local Tatar women selling healing herbs, and come to the eighth-century Uspensky Monastery (Assumption Monastery of the Caves), carved into the mountainside. Just enough light remains in the sky to illuminate the empty, broad, whitewashed steps leading up to its entrance.

Suddenly, as if startled by the sight of a large wading bird taking off unexpectedly across a smooth body of water, I stop in my tracks to watch an Orthodox priest in long black robes, crowned with a flat stovepipe hat, running toward and rapidly ascending all eighty-six steps. The sleeves of his gown, impersonating the bird's wings, spread out to the side and seem to launch him into flight. The billowing blackness of his ritual attire against the blank stillness of the bleached stairs takes my breath away.

Though exhausted, I wait a minute and climb up myself into the damp chapel cave, lit only by candles. Fearful of intruding, I stand at the back and listen to the mysterious, deep harmonies of the evening worship. The priests, made tall and imposing by their elevated headgear as well as by the folds of their robes, move effortlessly, like giant shadows, about the cave. Plato's parable drifts in and out of my consciousness, for it is these shadows that mediate my understanding. When the Soviets took control in 1921, they closed down this monastery. It was only in 1991, when the Ukrainians gained their independence, that it reopened—a history that recalls the fate of Foros Church as well as that of so many institutions victimized by Stalin's repressive measures.

That night, we arrive late at the Hotel Yalta—too late for the cavernous restaurant. The following day, tired of guides and wanting to see more of the Tatar culture, I alone take the funicular up to the 4,500-foot Mount Ai-Petri. On top are the Tatars, who descend from the Islamic groups that came to Crimea as early as the fifteenth century and eventually grew in numbers to comprise the largest ethnic group in the region. After stepping off the funicular, which climbs far above beech forests and juniper glades, I wander around open wild fields that make a sunken tabletop of the mountain and form a kind of basin that protects one from the wind. Scattered among the grasses of these measureless sea-meadows are paths that lead to places I don't have time to go, horses for riding, and tents in front of which wood fires grill meat and vegetables. I partake of the food and enjoy its freshness. From the sides of tables hang multiple strings of lush-looking, recently harvested red onions that people come from miles to buy, and on top stand rows of bottles containing lethal-looking homemade hard liquor. I am afraid to imbibe. Cooking and selling this food are rural, tough Tatars, darker in skin and hair than their customers. They are the survivors or descendants of a time, in May 1944, when the population of Crimean Tatars was forcibly deported and exiled to Central Asia. (The Soviets accused them of collaborating with the Nazis.) It was not until 1967 that the Crimean Tatars were rehabilitated but banned from legally returning to their homeland until the last days of the Soviet Union.

When I am enjoying a pleasant time on top of Mount Ai-Petri and among people enjoying the freshness of a mild day, I have no idea that after the Russian annexation of Crimea in 2014, these Tatars, of which there are over fifty thousand in Crimea, will once more be subject to hardship and violence. Many of their religious schools and homes will be searched under suspicion of possession of literature, which new Russian legislation labels extremist. Several Islamic books that were legal under Ukrainian law will be banned; the Crimean Tatars' religious and administrative buildings, as well as their homes, vandalized; and their language banned from schools.

Nor do I imagine, while strolling through the pastoral plains on top of this mountain, that thirty thousand Crimean Tatars will gather in the alpine meadow bowl on the upper plateau of Chatyr-Dah, close to the Simferopol-Alushta highway, to observe the seventieth anniversary of their deportation from Crimea. They will be forced to seek this mountain refuge, for Russian authorities will have forbidden commemorations elsewhere. Moreover, Crimean Tatar university students will be required to apply for a Russian passport and citizenship or else will not receive diplomas. In Bakhchysarai, a Crimean Tatar café called Musafir suspected of harboring "illegal" activity, will be searched by the Russian Federal Security Service.

Before leaving Crimea, I take a day to myself to wander along the coast near Yalta, just to see how far I can go and what I might find. Like the eponymous lady with the lapdog in Anton Chekhov's story set in Yalta, I, another Anna, here for the first time, promenade by the sea, but there is no Dmitry Dmitrich Gurov to gaze longingly at me.

The morning mist rises to join the white clouds lying motionless on the mountaintops. Not a leaf stirs on the trees, the cicadas chirp, and the sea, with its monotonous roar, reminds those who listen of the eternal sleep awaiting us all. Minutes and footsteps pass. A warming sun quietly brightens the prospect and with its harmonizing rays composes a pastorale. Along the beaches, sunbathers stretch as if removed from time. Farther along, from a tall cliff, I catch sight of naked bodies strewn blissfully on sands like mermaids waiting for some forbidden pleasure. Only occasionally do undertones of darkness intrude and change the tenor of the lyrical hours. On the surface, all looks peaceful and ideal, but death and war lurk in the moment as well as in the memory. I watch a stray cat stalking two hefty seagulls (the proportions are all wrong) and pause before a bed of petunias where inch-long insects, resembling hummingbirds and yearning for nectar in the death throes of their lives, are vibrating their wings and darting in and out of the flowers' trumpets. Nearby, floating in the sun, is the listless spirit of Chekhov who came to live here to cure his tuberculosis. In the distance, I see his estate and imagine I am there. The curtain rises to reveal the opening scene of *Uncle Vanya* set in a quiet garden compromised by conflict and thwarted desire.

ACT ONE: The garden. Part of the house and terrace can be seen. A table, laid for tea, stands on a path under an old poplar. Benches and chairs. There is a guitar on one of the benches. Near the table is a swing. It is between two and three o'clock in the afternoon.

Farther along, Livadia Palace—where Churchill, Roosevelt, and Stalin sat at a table to divide up Europe in 1945—looks out to a tranquil sea. On the way down through landscaped terraces, I meet a man accompanied by a clipped poodle and an eagle attached to his wrist. He provokes the two to quarrel and offers to place the eagle on my arm. Disgusted, I answer "*Nie.*"

Continuing, I arrive at the Alupka Palace, where Churchill stayed and where Rachmaninoff played. The structure strangely combines Edinburgh stone with Moorish ornamentation. On the way back, I bribe a gatekeeper to admit me through locked heavy gates to the Dyulber Sanatorium, built in the nineteenth century to resemble an Arabian palace. A nurse insists on showing me a suite of rooms where members of the Rada had recently stayed. They are luxuriously ornamented, a fantasy, yet oddly uncomfortable and unconvincing.

Time to go home. Back on the overnight train to Kiev, I succumb to the darkness and fall asleep. But it is not to be a peaceful slumber—what I feared on the way down becomes real. At 4:30 a.m., an intruder, who has a key to our private compartment, lets himself in and wakes me. He stands dark and tall at the end of my bunk. I see him because in reaching for the leather jacket I have hung at my feet, he mistakenly catches his arm on the light switch and then stands briefly illuminated in full view.

This accident saves my life, for earlier the attendant (who probably gave the intruder the key and told him who and where I was) said I should hide my valuables under my pillow. In the dark, the intruder would have come for these and either hit, gagged, or stabbed me. Strangely, this time I do not scream, but emitting some startled gasp, sit up straight. The man flees with my jacket. I wake up Irving, in the opposite bunk; we wonder what to do. The intruder must still be on the train.

Stupidly, like characters from Hitchcock's *The Lady Vanishes*, we furtively glance up and down the empty, narrow, rattling, dimly lit corridors; past windows that show nothing but the smudged raven darkness of early morning; past silent, blocked, locked doors; and naively search for any sight of him. Perhaps he has discarded the clothes that hide his invisibility and has become the invisible man from Orwell's novel, whom the man selling us newspapers on our train journey from Kiev to Crimea remembered and knew well. He has taken advantage of what the protagonist in *The Invisible Man* understands:

> We have to consider all that invisibility means, all
> that it does not mean. It means little advantage for
> eavesdropping and so forth—one makes sounds. It's
> of little help, a little help perhaps—in housebreaking
> and so forth. Once you've caught me you could
> easily imprison me. But on the other hand I am
> hard to catch. This invisibility, in fact, is only good
> in two cases: It's useful in getting away, it's useful
> in approaching. It's particularly useful, therefore, in
> killing. I can walk round a man, whatever weapon
> he has, choose my point, strike as I like. Dodge as I
> like. Escape as I like.

After much debate and confusion, Irving decides to look for our train attendant. He has to go through three train carriages before he finally spots an open compartment, complete with samovar, in which sits our attendant, jovially drinking steaming cups of black tea and gossiping with her friends. In Russian, he relates what has happened. Pretending disbelief, she hastily dons her uniform jacket over her corpulent figure and accompanies him back to our compartment where she plops heavily onto my bunk. Crying, wailing, and pretending to be sorry (as well as claiming she will lose her job), she offers to come to our apartment in Kiev to repay us for the lost leather jacket—an unreal proposition because someone on her salary could not possible afford to do this. She asks for our address and phone number. Just in time, I stop a rather-too-willing Irving from giving her our address—I imagine future complications, robberies, or bribes. Once back in Kiev she does phone, but Irving, thankfully, puts her off.

With this return, the embracing warmth and the illusion of peace in Crimea vanish all too abruptly—not a trace seems left. Such fantasies appear distant, even intangible, when we open the doors to 36 Bohdan Khmelnitski and learn that Yelena, our neighbor who has mothered and protected us since we arrived, has, during our absence, suddenly dropped dead. The morning is bleak and the day blank. The clouds that Irving, from our hotel room in Yalta, watched drift out to sea linger in anticipation of what is to come.

CHAPTER 7:

SHADOWS OF THE DEAD

BELARUS

Belarus is too close to Ukraine to resist, especially for Irving, whose mother and father spent the first twelve and fifteen years, respectively, of their lives in small, rural villages south of Minsk. Fleeing the threat of pogroms, as well as the dire economic conditions of the early 1900s, his parents, like many others, went to America where they later met and married.

During our tenure in Ukraine, we make two journeys to Belarus—the first at the end of May, the second toward the end of October—each for less than a week. These not only introduce us to a contemporary Belarus but also allow Irving to search for the landscape of his parents' childhoods. For this quest, he has only the names of villages that once drifted through his father's memory, descriptions of places from his deceased mother's autobiography (written in Yiddish), and a tattered photograph of a village funeral. These shadows of the dead are his imperfect guides. They do not promise much.

An invitation to lecture on contemporary American poetry at the European Humanities University in Minsk occasions the first trip in May. We take an overnight train to Minsk. The platform in Kiev is crowded with throngs of impoverished people who haul the hard trials of their lives in overstuffed, red-and-blue-striped plastic square bags that resemble bursting bales of hay. I have no idea where these passengers will put them or even how they have carried them. The plastic handles must cut, even into their calloused hands. After much scrambling, we reach our platform. The train arrives, and we are supposed to get into coach zero. Puzzled by the number that really is not a number, we wonder, *Is this real? Where does one find zero?* Running up and down the platform from one end of the train to the other, we discover that carriage zero is neither at the end of the train nor at its beginning. In this surreal world we have entered, zero does not precede one. Panic. Minutes before the train pulls out, we discover that zero comes between seven and eight. We jump on.

The journey lasts for thirteen arduous hours. We attempt to sleep but find it impossible, for in the process of crossing the border that separates Ukraine from Belarus, two sets of police (the Ukrainian and the Belarusian) board the train at midnight and again at 1:30 a.m., rudely wake us up by turning on the compartment light, and demand to examine our Belarusian visa and passport. Tense moments. The guards' shining, well-polished tall boots as well as their glossy pistol cases, slung across tight-fitting uniform jackets, evoke terrifying memories. I see some passengers being removed.

Bleary-eyed from the long journey from Kiev, we step off the train and walk into Minsk's monumental railroad station that, in the fog of breaking day, looms like some prehistoric monster out of a neoclassical swamp. Fog is everywhere, creeping, hovering, lying, and drooping. The mist and the pea-green industrial smog of the early morning curl through the openings between the station's tall Corinthian columns and into its cavernous, domed interior where hundreds and hundreds of bodies noiselessly swarm, stand, wander, or squat clustered in groups. The fog softens the harsh edges of their lives. As if already condemned to one of the circles of hell or anxiously anticipating some authoritative verdict, they silently await their fate. Large plastic containers, packed with most of their belongings, stand piled, waiting for someone to undo them. The last line of Matthew Arnold's "The Scholar Gypsy" comes to mind: "the dark Iberians come; / And on the beach undid his corded bales."

Lost among this multitude of tortured, dead souls and confused by the labyrinthine corridors that are conduits for the swirling haze, we stand stunned. A single lightbulb hangs from the ceiling and does little to aid us. Think of the whole of Euston Station or Grand Central lit by one dim bulb. We are supposed to meet a guide, but how? No exit. No place. Irving decides to go on a pilgrimage in search of the man (whose identity is unknown). Fortune is nearby, for after about fifteen minutes he returns with a fur-capped driver-guide in tow. It is a miracle. Soon, in the clearer light of midmorning, we are driving through Minsk, a city that lacks the intimate, ornamental, and extensive beauty of Kiev.

During World War II, Minsk was bombed, burned, and flattened, so there is little that is old. Minsk is now a horizontal, new city, spread out and deliberately divided into commanding, charted lines. Gaping spaces between buildings and heavy Russian-style monuments oppress the viewer and, for a moment, remind one of a history of destruction and continuing occupation. Traveling from the Minsk Railroad Station to the Hotel Jubliana is particularly surreal, for the disparity between the visible present and an eradicated past is extreme and unbridgeable.

Persuaded by the bustling, eager present, one perhaps too easily forgets that supporters of Stalin's repression, Soviet partisans, members of the resistance movements, mass murderers,

marauding auxiliary police, SS officers, and displaced minorities once actually trod these streets and were the perpetrators or victims of terror. New buildings obliterate memories of utter devastating destruction. And the sight of present-day crowds walking, shopping, taking the buses, driving their cars, and generally going about their ordinary business contradicts the horrendous fact that not so many years ago, Belarus lost a quarter of its prewar inhabitants, including 90 percent of its Jewish population. After that, writers and intellectuals disappeared under Stalinism. (In the Old Town of Minsk, there is a museum dedicated to these writers and thinkers.)

To negotiate these realities is difficult, uncomfortable, if not impossible. In many ways, it is easier simply to lose oneself in the present. If I am to be honest, for this reason in the days ahead I am sometimes impatient during our journey to locate the landscape of the past. In fairness, however, I should acknowledge that as much as Irving is intent upon finding the villages, he is just as committed as I to engaging the present. In particular, for both of us, the time spent with the university students is memorable. Their dogged, lively curiosity, which seems to be a continuation of the intellectual flavor of Minsk before the Second World War "cleansed" the city of most of its scholarly and creative elite, is moving and reassuring.

In May 2000, we enter at a time when an increasingly isolated Belarus is more and more subject to Russia's demands. Russian has officially been declared to be on equal footing with the Belarusian language and is now the dominant tongue. Russia controls the economy. (Belarus is integrated into the Russian Federation.) Belarus's president, Alexander Lukashenko, a supporter of the Soviets, has been in power for six years. His rule is popularly referred to as "the last dictatorship" in Europe. He heads a government (though technically a democracy since 1999) that exerts tight control over institutions and the national press. Among thousands of repercussions, the curriculum in higher education suffers. Soon the American Studies program at the European Humanities University, a private university founded in 1992, where I am to lecture in Minsk, will disappear. Students eager to engage Western philosophical and literary thought will be pressured to shift their attention to Eastern European culture, science, business, and technology. Just three years later, the university's president will be called before the Belarusian education minister and told to resign. And then, in a few months, the university itself will be expelled from Belarus and will relocate across the border in Lithuania.

UGLÍ, UGLOO, UGLOV

When the conference in Minsk at the European Humanities University comes to an end, we turn our attention to finding the villages where Irving's parents were born. After innumerable phone calls and trips to and from a well-meaning travel agency (Irving's request to find his Jewish family's roots is the agency's first attempt to do anything like this), we sit and talk with those who are willing to help. At first neither of us has confidence that the search is realistic. We consult maps (some of which display "red zones" for high nuclear deposits and many of which reveal that there are seventeen places called Uglí—a name that simply means "corners"). After confronting the reality that names of streets and villages are not only repetitive but also variable (for instance, if one is going to Uglí, one is going to Ugloo, and if one is coming from Uglí, one is coming from Uglov), all seems speculative and a little fantastic. The quest evokes memories of our almost futile attempt to find the correct train carriage to transport us from Kiev to Minsk. Names as well as numbers shift and, like Proteus, as soon as one tries to take hold of them, morph into other shapes or sequences to frustrate the desire to arrive and grasp what one reaches for.

Encouraged by our guide, we start out anyway—toward an area near one of the many Uglís. Traveling south into the countryside from Minsk is an immediate experience. There is no transition: no suburb, no industry, just suddenly fields. The road out of the city is straight. At one point, the police block our way. We pay a bribe and continue. Unlike the thick, cold fog of yesterday's arrival, the weather is now cloudless, hot, and sticky, so the driver halts at a little shop, buys a bottled drink, and agrees to give a woman a ride to her village. The bus goes through only once a day.

The first village we come to is, if the map is to be believed, probably Doktoworich, the village where Irving's father was born. No sign announces its identity, but when the driver inquires, a man walking down the road replies, "*Da*, Doktoworich." When Irving hears this local person pronounce the name (the speaker puts the emphasis on the first syllable rather than on the second), he realizes he is listening to the name just as his father and his maternal grandfather pronounced it—a first clue, perhaps, that this is the right area. In old Doktoworich, we manage to find the Soviet, the regional office, where the secretary (already contacted by the travel agency) joins us and tries her best to help. Irving mentions two other villages (Uglí and Stanki) that his parents used to talk about. We consult a map we have brought along but do not find either Uglí or Stanki. Determined to continue, we get in the car and, within a few miles, believe it or not, notice a sign for Stanki, and then in a few kilometers, one for Uglí.

The close proximity of Doktoworich, Stanki, and Uglí suddenly makes this quest real. The burned site of a tavern also adds to the probability. Irving's grandfather ran a tavern. We convince ourselves that we are in the right locale and have arrived in yet another place where the invisible past almost metamorphoses into visibility. Spontaneously, my mind returns to the huddled displaced bodies at the Minsk train station. Their dim silhouettes merge with the ghostly landscape in front of us and remind me that German troops once burned and murdered their way through this area.

The secretary takes Irving to meet elderly people, hoping that they might remember the Jewish population in these villages. (Few young remain—they leave for the cities. A motorbike parked outside a house is a sign that a young man lives there.) Irving realizes, of course, that there is no chance that anybody might know or have heard of descendents of his family who remained and survived after his parents' departure in the early 1900s. He is introduced to a ninety-two-year-old lady and an aged man (age either unknown or forgotten). Both are deaf (except when the man's cow gets loose, he hears it perfectly and runs out to fetch it). The secretary gently shouts questions, for which there are few answers, if any. The two recall seeing a young Jewish girl being dragged from a house across the street and murdered by the Nazi troops. But that is all.

The history Irving is curious about has either, at least in the text of their lives, never existed or been erased. The more recent atrocities are remembered with shame and therefore censored. Reluctant to acknowledge what remains, these villagers have repressed as much as they can. Irving decides not to pursue. Indeed, it is a relief to turn away from the past, for Irving is having difficulty imagining that this village was once where his mother lived. As it stands now, its buildings, its layout, its people bear little resemblance to the region she describes in her autobiography. Nothing mirrors her memory. The traditional log cabins (shown in Irving's one photograph) that once circled a village green are gone (the one remaining example is decaying and falling down) and are replaced by ordinary wooden bungalows. The culture has disappeared, Yiddish is silent, and the inhabitants changed.

For Irving, the villages are disappointing. To him they look barren, drab, and flat. I, on the other hand, unescorted by filial remembrance and, for the moment, repressing the region's history, cast my eyes on dwellings fronted by lush vegetable and flower gardens, blossoming fruit trees, and colorful picket fences that seem to create an idyllic picture. Just beyond these fences are wooden benches where the old people sit and where the barefooted rest. In front of every two houses are deep wells full of spring water, cold and sweet, which comes up in buckets attached to a long wooden pole that one swings or presses down to dip into the well. Two or three times a day, cows stroll down the dirt road to and from the feeding pasture. A woman or a man with a twig follows and occasionally encourages a recalcitrant animal to move on. On their return, the cows know which house or yard to enter. They turn slowly, deliberately, dutifully into their stalls. Around each dwelling, chickens and goslings rest in the shade or, like bleached leaves blown in autumn, scatter across the road. Attached to the houses are small wooden pens out of which the snouts of pigs catch the scent. I stop to say a few words to the pigs. A blurry-eyed man, wiry and humorous, wobbles over and jests, "You came all this way and spent a lot of money just to see pigs!" (He has a point.) Ducks perch on top of fences, and tied dogs bark, wag their tails, and pose for their photograph.

After the awkwardness of the references to the Holocaust, once the conversation turns more willingly to the immediate surroundings, the villagers (and I, too) are more relaxed. Neighbors hand me flowers and invite us inside their homes. Just before we depart, however, we accidentally unearth a raw vein running through the topography of their seemingly pastoral lives. And that is when Irving turns his attention to a ragged workhorse attached to a farmer's wooden cart.

Curious about what seems to be an unusually arched yoke above the horse's head, he appreciatively points and asks our guide about its design. Startled, the nag's owner, who has been jealously monitoring Irving's interest, angrily rushes up, fists

ready to strike. In his eyes, Irving, as outsider, is a gypsy and means to steal his horse. After reassuring words from people who have gathered to witness and mediate the altercation, the owner departs, but unconvinced. Paradoxically, when we are on the way back to Minsk, a gypsy stops our car. He pretends he has lost his way and tries to sell us a "gold ring." Tit for tat.

Exhausted at the end of this day, we cross the checkpoint into Minsk. Afterimages of the countryside and farmlands quarrel with the cityscape's avenues of concrete multistory buildings and illuminated pavements visible through the van's window. The two prospects are as incompatible as the past and the present. Thinking that there might be more to learn, we consider returning another time.

BELARUS, 2000

The second trip to Belarus, in the cold month of October, 2000, is more efficient, systematic, and "scientific." The freezing weather now tempers the heat of novelty. This time a Jewish agency (composed of a young, ambitious Jewish couple) that specializes in helping people locate their roots is in charge. They have arranged for Irving to meet with archivists and to visit old Jewish cemeteries, where possibly his mother's family is buried.

This time we fly rather than endure the thirteen-hour train trip. And with us is the elderly, vain, and rather lopsided, bent-backed widow of Irving's cousin. (I wait for hours every morning while she arranges her thin wisps of hair into a style she wore when she was beautiful.) She has come over from Canada especially to learn more about her deceased husband's roots. We fly to Minsk via Belavion, a Belarusian airline that specializes in acquiring discarded planes from the Russians. The flight departs from the Kiev national airport (close to the center), which resembles a run-down 1950s Trailways Station I once knew well in Charlottesville, Virginia. We are in the wrong place! Is this actually a terminal? But it is.

A van drawn by an old yellow truck transports passengers to the planes, which some call "flying tractors." Each holds about fifty passengers, is solid, and flies at extremely low altitudes (not far to fall, I think). The interior is straight out of the '50s: aquamarine decorations, wide leather seats, broad aisles, and vanity mirrors (Irving's relative tidies her hair again). We rumble off on tires that seem to have been stolen from a Tonka truck and, strange to say, begin one of the most comfortable flights I have ever experienced.

Knowing the flight route will take us over the Chernobyl nuclear reactors, I keep my eyes glued to the window. Suddenly, 1986 comes into view. The brilliantly clear day and the plane's low altitude make it possible, unbelievably, to see the silent tall abandoned chimneys extending their concrete fingers, as if wanting to stroke the plane's belly and reestablish a contact that is now forbidden. I look at the wrecked buildings, the smoke still spewing from a barely functioning reactor, the polluted Dnieper River (or Soz River) gurgling inappropriately next to the ruins, the adjoining scarred landscape, and the deserted town. How disturbingly appealing the site is, and how odd to know that people continue to enter these poisoned areas not just to try to contain the leaking radiation but also to poach and to plunder. The area around Chernobyl is supposed now to be a good hunting ground.

An hour and twenty minutes later, the plane lands in Minsk. Waiting in line for passport control is a former dean of the library school in Boston. He is soon whisked away by the US embassy officials. There is also a German professor of business, who admits to me that he is a missionary disguised as an academic. He tells me that because missionaries are forbidden in Belarus, they must come in on other pretexts. He, consequently, teaches business from a Christian perspective. Evangelicals like him are a thorn in the side of Eastern Europe.

The guide for this second visit is where she says she will be. She takes us to the Hotel Minsk. One look at its drab, dangling lamps, its dull brown walls, towels, carpets, cigarette-holed bed covers, natty curtains, and at its excessively narrow beds convinces me that we should move to the Hotel Jubliana, where we stayed before. Two leather-jacketed thugs trashing the room next door clinch my determination to move.

At the Hotel Jubliana, Irving's relative is, thankfully, assigned the only remaining "Western" single room. She will be comfortable. We climb up stairs to another floor where there are "Soviet-style rooms," which, although still a bit on the brown, frumpy side, are superior to what the Hotel Minsk offers. At first, no hot water runs through our taps. We call a willing but drunk maintenance man, who says we should let the water run for twenty minutes to allow the hot water to reach our room. We try but find only a lukewarm offering. Another ten minutes pass, and the water reverts to its icy origins. The heat is not on, either. I consider calling for a hot-water bottle to warm the damp sheets. Strangely, what runs through my mind is the fact that on September 22, 1943, an SS officer, Wilhelm Kube, made a similar request. The hotel maid promptly came to his room and put the hot water bottle in his bed; however, when the officer crawled under the blankets, the container blew up and mangled him. The maid, either a partisan or an enemy, had placed a bomb inside the bottle. (In Minsk, this officer had thrown sweets to Jewish children who had been tossed into a deep pit of sand. His absurd act was his strange attempt to silence their terrified and failing cries.) Tomorrow, things will be better, we trust, and, for the moment, they are. There is not only hot water but also heat.

In the morning we drive in a van supplied by our guide to Kapyl (*Kapulye* in Yiddish), a town with a Jewish cemetery and a regional archive, which the Soviets established after World War II, when they required each region to compile records of its history and its people. One result is that there are now meticulously collected records of all inhabitants, dead and alive. Alone in the back of the van and hiding from the ceaseless anticipatory chatter among the guide, Irving, and his relative, I watch the morning sun illuminate and melt the previous night's hoar frost. Its golden light settles on tall silver birches, glazes the streams, gilds the poplar leaves, which cluster and shake like precious coins waiting to be spent, and warms the white soil. Some think the name Belarus comes from the pale color of its soil.

In Kapyl, we stumble through a lumpy, exposed field among the jumbled and overgrown remains of the Jewish graves. Some Hebraic writing is still visible, but most is washed away by the wind, rain, and time. I learn that in old cemeteries within forests the inscriptions, protected by the trees, remain longer. A cow chews the grass and a child, put in charge of it, occasionally pulls on its tether. Realizing the impossibility of this exercise, we halfheartedly pull weeds off the few intact gravestones and with a whisk brush attempt to clear away the algae and dust from the fading letters. Irving was hoping to find his mother's family's name, but all remains as elusive and unknowable as ever. From the field, we walk over to the regional museum—which is, like all public buildings, under *remont* (renovation). It is locked. After a few despondent minutes, I catch sight of a young woman, carrying her Saturday shopping and heading toward us. She is the curator returning from her lunch break. Her genuine interest in the Jewish past is absolutely astonishing.

For the next two interminable hours, the guide, Irving, and his relative—engrossed in their task and in the grip of memory—huddle together in a small, unheated office, examining papers from the Soviet archives. Hunched in an attempt to keep what body heat remains under my coat and scarf (even the curator wears a thick vest and lined boots), I sit apart in a corner, next to an ancient typewriter, and watch them painstakingly go over lists of names and through handwritten documents I don't understand and that the eager curator keeps bringing in from other rooms and out of packed files. She finds many references and papers having to do with Mendele Mokher Sforim, a relative of Irving's mother. Some consider him the founder of Yiddish fiction. Finally, there is some actual, concrete evidence that people Irving's mother mentions in her autobiography lived in this region.

The curator continues to be helpful. She finds the telephone number of a surviving Jew in Kapyl. She calls; a person answers only to tell her that Mr. Abromowich (meaning "book peddler") has left for the market in another town and will not be back until the next morning. A meeting will not be feasible. As if to compensate for the disappointment, the curator tells Irving about a memorial book, compiled from government documents, published in Minsk. The publication exhaustively lists the names of all the people murdered by the Nazis in the Kapyl region. Years later, the tome arrives in Buffalo, courtesy of a friend from Kiev who has traveled to Minsk. Up to that point, purchasing a copy has been impossible. An isolated Minsk does not take checks, credit cards, postal orders, or anything we can think of.

The morning has been fruitful. Satisfaction, however, strangely and disappointingly does not, in my present, slightly ungenerous state of mind, compensate for the hunger and the biting cold that gnaw on every part of my body. Now that names are found, I simply want to leave and seek relief from the freezing air that contributes to my weariness. Finally, we cross the street to a depressing cafeteria where I devour an aged cutlet and raw rice.

Back in the van, we return to the villages Uglí and Stanki. I am, however, eager to see them again. I think of the first time when, in May, the sight of these villages stimulated my sentimental imagination and evoked idyllic images of nineteenth-century rural communities. Returning in the winter breaks this illusion. Now the gilt frame of the picturesque scene is shattered and the canvas damaged. Instead of seeing elderly people sitting in the serenity of the sun, I notice people tramping through mud and muck in galoshes, thick stockings, and bulky coats. The roads that arrange each village don't meander; they are straight and wide—regulated. The houses are badly constructed. The population that works the land, as well as the collective farms, toils hard. People's hands are the large, muscular appendages of laborers; their bodies are burly; their faces round with brilliant blue eyes; and their skin red-cheeked and scarred from the drudge of their lives.

They remember us. Talkative groups of men and women gather to escort us from house to house. One particularly bent woman, leaning on her stick, leads the way. With her gold-capped teeth, she chews a raw onion and takes us to meet an eighty-nine-year-old woman who stands as straight as a broom. I step into the warmth of kitchens where old-fashioned tiled stoves offer shelves for sleeping (lovely and warm) and ovens for baking. One woman fills my pockets with roasted pumpkin seeds she has removed from the oven with a long wooden paddle. On top of her stove, a stew simmers in an iron pot. I venture into a homemade sauna that a young man is eager to show off. In other dwellings are cabbages piled and stored in cold spaces; apples laid out to dry (their sweet and healing fragrance permeating the room); photographs of lost sons, daughters, and husbands; folk icons propped in a corner; ceremoniously embroidered hanging cloths; celebratory posters of Lenin taped to the wall (the elderly admire the old Soviet system); and platters of late-season bruised pears.

One lady fills my backpack with several dozen. In a cottage where we drink steaming tea, an old woman opens a trunk and carefully pulls out a tablecloth. It belonged to her wedding trousseau. She despairs, "What can I do with this now?" Does she want us to buy it? Does it mean her family has gone? As in so many other instances, we are not sure, so simply admire its

exquisite stitching. We listen to stories of their lives, some sad. One woman's husband has just suffered a heart attack, and now she is left with an alcoholic son. I also overhear declarations that I wish were not uttered: "The Jews were nice, like the Russians." It is impossible to understand or respond to these.

It is time to leave. The horse wagons with their arched yokes pass us by. I gaze at the stork's nest above the grounds of the collective farm. In the evening, the stork perches on an electric pole and looks down upon the blushing haze of the setting sun. Farther down the dirt road is a wide-open, damp, shadowed field of muck in which groups of young people are spread and bent, sorting potatoes with their chapped, raw fingers.

One evening, the guides from the Jewish agency come over to our hotel in Minsk. We meet in the lobby—an empty brown lounge—and for the next four hours listen to stories of survival they have heard various customers relate. One narrative is about a man who, when he was six, ran away from the ghetto in Minsk. After hiding in the woods, he was recaptured. On the eve of his execution, Latvian officers adopted him as a mascot and errand boy. For months, these officers took him with them to the killing fields. After the war, the young boy found his way to Australia, where he was placed alone in the wilderness. His job was to man a railway crossing. Every few months, the train dropped off food and supplies for his survival. Not being able to take this solitude anymore, he jumped on a circus train that happened to be coming along the tracks. For years, he worked in the circus. Like so many narratives of survival, the story of his nomadic life continues and at one point brings him back to Minsk.

While Irving, his relative, and the guides, seated in a closed circle, chat away for hours, absorbed by these stories, my attention starts to wander toward what was an empty bar that is now filling up with prostitutes and German businessmen. It is beyond midnight. The stories continue and those who listen don't see the gamblers going to and from the hotel's casino. Oblivious to their immediate surroundings and the dimly lit present, neither Irving nor his cousin nor the guides notice that two leather-jacketed young men are trying to race into the hotel through automatic sliding doors that move too slowly for their pace. The men run right smash into the doors and fall to the ground; muscular security guards and padded armed militia (who seem to emerge from nowhere) race commandingly toward them. Outside the hotel entrance, they and their violence vanish into the darkness and silence of night and forgetfulness. I never see any of them again. The compelling past, though poorly lit, remains inside, anecdotally recalled and partially visible.

The national airport in Minsk mimics a Greek temple on the outside but within resembles a deserted marble tomb, cracked, empty, and drafty. The flight is delayed three hours, so we sit on plastic chairs. The toilet is under *remont* so is not available; the café is open. Cockroaches run among the open-faced sandwiches. Amusingly some of the customers play with them. Irving's cousin (she escaped from a village in Poland just before the Nazi occupation) becomes anxious as if all the memories and ghosts are assembled here. She cannot find her visa. And when a customs official tries to help her with her heavy suitcase, she cannot believe that he is not inspecting, judging, condemning, or even taking her away. There ensues a tug-of-war that, if it were not tragic, would be absurdly comic. Bent over, her long, full dress almost reaching the floor and her jewelry swinging defiantly, she clings determinedly to the suitcase handles, as if holding on to the last breaths of life. She pulls away from the uniformed official, who politely yet firmly attempts to take it from her resolute fingers so he might place the case on the conveyer belt. Only when we rush forward and put a stop to the struggle, like referees in a boxing match, does she give up. For her, at this moment, the past overwhelms the present and blinds her to what is really going on.

Upon our return, Kiev, in contrast to Minsk, looks even more splendid, bright, and stylish than it did before we left.

CHAPTER 8:

THE LEAVING

November arrives, the days grow shorter, and so does my time in Ukraine. I shall be leaving mid-December. The moment of departure draws closer and closer. We must return to Buffalo. Speeches, presents, group photographs, and promises fill our last week. At the airport, Natalia and Tamara see us off. Leaning over the railing dividing us, our friends watch us place our bulging bags on the conveyer belt. Our eyes touch. In a few minutes, after one last turn of the head, we must move on, knowing that we will never see each other again.

Endings bring with them a certain madness. Mine takes the form of an overwhelming impulse to collect nineteenth-century Ukrainian icons and smuggle them home. (For this reason, I never buy one that has metal on it for the airport X-ray machines will find me out.) Even though I am not religious, the sacred icon held high above the priest's head in Odessa strangely haunts my consciousness, as do others that have become phantoms in my memory. These images carry with them the feelings and habits of those who created them. Rendered by a living, imperfect hand, each contains a still moment of desire for rest and salvation in a long history of conflict, conquest, and difficulty.

Knowing that displaced, stolen, and damaged icons are on the market, my quest leads to antique stalls lining the roughly cobbled Andriyivsky Descent (Kiev's Montmartre), which winds to the lower city, past Mikhail Bulgakov's house where he wrote *The White Guards*—a novel, set in late 1918, about a family caught up in the various factions (the Whites, the Reds, the Imperial German Army, and the Ukrainian nationalists) that pummel, divide, and destroy their world. As I write, I cannot help but think of the eastern Ukrainians in cities such as Luhansk and Donetsk, split between loyalties and survival, divided among themselves. Those who have not been able to leave and live with relatives elsewhere are caught in basements, afraid to go out, for fear of being bombed or rounded up. Their pensions cut off, they wait for bread lines and food kitchens. On the border between Ukraine and Russia during "cease fires" of a never-ending war, explosives fall between already-ruined buildings.

Continuing my search for the displaced, I rummage through makeshift booths set up for a day (at one I find a heavily varnished St. Michael propped on a suitcase fashioned into a table). In the courtyard behind my apartment, I enter a jewelry shop to consider buying a folk icon hanging behind the counter. (Some family has discarded it.) Farther down, I come to a set of broad steps, leading to a higher street, where thick-coated and gloved people, in an attempt to earn a few pennies, sell "treasures" from their home. I find nothing but do meet a man who promises to restore damaged icons for a few pennies.

One day I read about a gathering of antique collectors, who meet every Saturday morning in a cavernous nightclub, appropriately named the New York Club. We are determined to find

it, rain or shine. The day we decide to go, it is raining, a heavy, penetrating, deep-puddled downpour. Having no address but the New York Club, we are not sure where to go, but the shopkeeper in our neighborhood jewelry shop does. Off we go via the metro underground across the river. Half an hour later, in an alien residential district, we ask anyone who passes by where the club might be. Eventually, a saturated drunk with a swollen eye leads us in zigzags through nasty concrete apartment courtyards, around corners, and across a muddy park to our destination. Outside the club, like crows standing around fresh roadkill, leather-jacketed, short-cropped male figures consider their next moves. Smoke from their cigarettes swirls cannily through their dealings and the wet. Occasionally a male figure with a painting tucked under his arm or an ancient light fixture in a plastic carrier bag hastily leaves the building like a slanted shadow blown across an open square.

When we enter, the darkness in the club is blinding. The only light comes from either a buffet bar or a tiny wicket, where we buy an entrance ticket from a fur-hatted, stout matron whose chubby fingers sport amber rings. With difficulty, we grope our way to the silhouette of a disco floor around which dealers' tables, arranged in three immense circles, create a maze of treasures. Even though an occasional lamp exposes a detail or two, it is too dark to see anything properly. An abandoned, unlit, revolving sparkling light dangles from the center of the ceiling and fails to expose the Minotaur that surely waits patiently for its prey in the center of this labyrinth. Behind each table men display, exchange, and sell their chaotic heaps of wares: collections of medals, photographs, paintings, icons, china pieces, and jewelry. The atmosphere is serious, hushed, and subdued. I am one of only a few women here. This is a man's world. For two hours, until closing time, we roam this den of thieves and work our way through this Bosch-like cavity. I leave with two icons (neither of which I can really see). One is a fine icon from western Ukraine; the other, a lively St. George crawling with wormholes—the man on the steps will fix those in a week's time.

Damp and tired, we duck into a warm café and then spend two more hours, this time in an open market, looking for hand-knit wool socks. To make sure they are the correct size, the merchant has Irving make his hand into a fist and see if it will get easily into the sock. Ingenuity. I am reminded of when I buy black woolen tights from a stand on the street outside the apartment. The lady takes one look at me (even in a coat) and immediately knows the right size. She is always accurate.

Time passes; I am at the airport to fly back to the States. The socks and the sequestered icons (I have given away most of my clothes to make room for these) glide unnoticed through the X-ray machine and will return with me. The matriarchal society of room 73 leans over a banister separating visitors and departing passengers. We throw kisses, promises, and longing looks. I don't want to let go of this past year, but as the plane moves closer to the West and the chatter up and down the aisles surreptitiously and cautiously shifts to English, all starts to be jumbled. (Where am I?) Like Alice at the conclusion of *Alice Through the Looking Glass*, I cannot help but pull out the tablecloth from beneath all that has been set upon it during the previous months so that everything tumbles and scatters: people, places, incidents, images, and words begin to fall away and change shape. What once so clearly and definitively classified my life in Ukraine disappointingly starts slipping into some dreamlike state. The taxonomy of my surroundings shifts back to a previous schema. Everything around me begins to revert to the familiar, yet foreign, profile of home. The Red and White Queens become ordinary domestic cats. I am grateful to be met in London by Celia who, because she visited me in Kiev, can affirm that where I have been and what I have seen are real. Standing in line at passport control, I find it momentarily reassuring to overhear, as well as partially understand, two Ukrainians converse behind me. Though their talk is commonplace, their presence is not.

AFTERWORD:

THE ARCHIVES AND DR. NOVAK

Two decades after my return from Ukraine, the figures of Dr. Novak, Ludik Benes, and Mrs. Kessler from my childhood continue to haunt my mind. In spite of the tender feelings that grace my remembrance of them, their increasingly fragile presence is disquieting, for there is still much I do not know about their lives during the time I was living in the parsonage a few miles from Manchester. I keep wondering, what exactly did Dr. Novak see in Prague in 1945 and 1946, before he visited my family? What happened to Ludik Benes once he left the 1946 IRA conference in Manchester and returned home? And what did Mrs. Kessler endure before she landed in England in 1947?

In an attempt to answer these unsolvable questions, I recently embarked on yet another journey. This time I was not to board a plane; rather, I was to travel virtually to the digital archives of the Unitarian Service Committee, housed in the Harvard Divinity School library. Because Dr. Novak and Ludik Benes belonged to the Unitarian movement, I trusted that the postwar documents in these archives, especially those having to do with Czechoslovakia, might reveal something about the circumstances of their lives and perhaps might even mention their names. Alas, and perhaps predictably, I found no reference to their names, but I did discover raw materials that bluntly portray what an individual living in Prague might have known or seen right after the end of the war. Even though I did not learn anything specifically about my childhood acquaintances, I did come away with a more definitive sense of the distressing, and often threatening, situations that challenged their lives from 1945 to 1950. Reading through these papers, I came to understand that bombed-out Manchester, in comparison with the human suffering and condition of their home country, must have looked like paradise. I also gained a more vivid sense than I already possessed of just how horrific the environment Mrs. Kessler survived had been.

What follow are a few of these documents.

Among the most poignant letters in the Unitarian Service Committee files is a letter sent from Prague, dated May 29, 1945, to "friends" in the West just twenty days after the liberation by the Soviets of the Theresienstadt ghetto, a concentration camp in northwest Czechoslovakia. Composed after "years of compelled silence," this elegant missive proffers a devastating account of some of the chaotic and dire difficulties in Czechoslovakia right after the war. The letter bears no signature but appears to have been written by a well-educated European, residing in Prague, who was dedicated to and in a position to seek assistance. (The few unidiomatic expressions demonstrate that the writer is not a native English speaker.) Whether or not he was hired by the Unitarian Service Committee, I do not know.

Though the letter's details offer an outline and no more of the larger grief, they catch the essence of the horrific state of affairs that must have been all too familiar to those whom I met in my early childhood and who up to this point must have also lived under the weight of what the correspondent calls "a compelled silence." This anonymous May, 1945, letter begins:

> *Dear Friends, I am so glad to be able to send you a message after years of compelled silence. Our thoughts have often been with you all and our hearts beat high when we heard in your radio a few days before the revolution that you were present at a reception of the new Czechoslovak minister at Zürich.*

The correspondent continues by isolating some of the dire problems following the release of three hundred thousand workers and prisoners from concentration camps in Czechoslovakia as well as from other parts of Europe, who are now attempting to return to their home country. In particular, he mentions Theresienstadt, which the Nazis ran as a showpiece and which housed many children. In reality, Theresienstadt was used as both a labor and a transit camp for Czech Jews who were deported either to killing centers or to forced-labor camps in German-occupied Poland, Belarus, and the Baltic States.

> *Our social work has not been interrupted and now it has to grow enormously. P. has initiated and is leading the organization of four recovery homes for children from Theresienstadt in confiscated castles, in collaboration with the ministries of health and repatriation. There are very many obstacles and even the best organized services would never be able to master the enormous problems that the postwar conditions heap upon this country. Among the worst*

is the fact that three hundred thousand exported
workers and prisoners are flooding back from all
sides in a very poor physical, mental and moral state
into their home country with the hope of finding
paradise after years of privation, in fact finding
a robbed-out country disorganized after a long
occupation and the excesses of revolution.

In particular, the writer draws attention to the dire circumstances facing foreign civil prisoners, who are still on Czech soil, especially the foreign Jews at Theresienstadt. Perhaps Mrs. Kessler was among them:

This old little "ville de garrison" [Theresienstadt],
which used to have a population of seven thousand,
including the soldiers was all turned into one ghetto
by the Nazis and is still lodging thirty thousand
Jews of many nationalities. Not long ago it had sixty
thousand inhabitants, most of which have been
killed. The sanitary and food conditions are being
improved now, but lodging is still very bad.

What the writer of this letter finds especially upsetting are the children who have just been released from Theresienstadt. Many are in terrible condition, physically and emotionally:

I was there a week ago, when we brought out the
first group of orphans to the castle that was first
quickly "adapted" in a few days. I saw a room of
about thirty square meters in which twenty-seven
boys of twelve to sixteen live day and night in a
state of general apathy. They have been transported
here worse than cattle during the last weeks
before capitulation from concentration camps

that the Germans evacuated before the enemy.
These boys most look like skeletons covered with
yellow skin, many of them with faces of old men.
There are still about five hundred such boys at
Th. [Theresienstadt], mostly Polish. Very many
have died on the way and some are still dying. The
children that have been only at Th., not in other
concentration camps, look much better, but badly
need mental recovery. We hope, in spite of many
psychological difficulties, to improve the near future
for most of them, but the authorities are interested
in sending them as soon as possible back into their
countries of origin.

The correspondent's anguish is prompted not just by the children's condition but also because they have nothing to return to except, as he acknowledges, the reality of a still-active anti-Semitism. As he astutely remarks: "anti-Semitism has not died with Hitler":

Now this is the saddest part of their fate: to be sent
back into a country absolutely ruined where they
have neither relatives nor friends left and where no
one will be interested to help them because anti-
Semitism has not died with Hitler. It is especially the
case with these shadows of Polish boys, but in lesser
degree also with many Germans. There are still five
thousand Jews from Germany in Th. Over a fifth of
them have no one left in Germany and dread the
return to such an inhospitable place.

Concerned because of a lack of organization and communication among agencies supposed to be offering relief, and sensitive as well to the fact that "the population is longing more for rest than for work," he worries that "very little is done for the future of all foreign Jews." He despairs:

> *Please, do something about it! Give a copy of this with necessary recommendation to the I.R.C. [International Relief Committee] at Geneva and any organizations likely to be able to do something about offers of hospitality. Of course help of any kind must be offered or mediated by some organization that enjoys a certain consideration with the present chief ally of this country. Mere financial help is of no avail as private initiative here has no possibilities in this field.*
> —Harvard Divinity School library. bms 16035/1 (17).

Through further research, I discovered that "P.," the man referred to in the second quotation from the above letter, is probably Policer, a Hungarian Jew who in 1945 was appointed by Noel Field, the European director of the rescue mission of the Unitarian Service Committee, to direct the Czechoslovak chapter.[1] The two met in Marseilles, where Field had collaborated with a French Jewish humanitarian organization to provide relief for endangered Jewish refugees. When he accepted this position, Policer changed his name to Dr. Gejza Pavlik. (He altered his surname in order to disguise his ethnicity and sound more Slavic.)

Pavlik's job lasted only until mid-1946. During that period, he and his wife, Charlotte, who had worked with refugees in Geneva, succeeded, with the assistance of the Unitarian Service Committee, in getting homes for orphaned or displaced children and organizing medical treatment centers. During that period, Pavlik wrote four reports for the USC in which he described the economic and social problems facing

---

1. *Field was appointed European Director of the Rescue Mission of the USC in late 1942 or early 1943.*

postwar Czechoslovakia. A selection from one of these reports, describing the general conditions in the country, is quoted in a letter prepared in December 1945 and sent from the Hotel Alcron in Prague by an unnamed correspondent. (Again, this document is unsigned, but I believe it was submitted by Field, who hired Pavlik.) The paragraph from Pavlik's report, inserted into this letter, describes the appalling circumstances of most living in Czechoslovakia.

> *The situation is frequently sadder than one could imagine. The occupation and the war have left the most sinister consequences. The feeding of the urban population in meat, milk, fats is an especially serious problem. The Germans have killed practically all the cattle. This year's harvest was bad. Wherever the fighting has passed the homes have been largely destroyed. In the eastern portion of Slovakia there are 5,000 (?) people without any homes whatever. The public authorities attempt to bring help, but as transportation is lacking, all efforts move too slowly. To understand the situation it is only necessary to remember that the Germans have removed or destroyed 50 percent of the locomotives, they have blown up all of the railway bridges, they have even removed hundreds of kilometers of rails, repair shops have been completely destroyed, etc., etc. So in spite of the efforts of the authorities, a large part of the war victims will remain without shelter during the winter.*
> —Harvard Divinity School library.
> bms 16035 (9) seq. 10.

By 1946, when Dr. Novak and Ludik Benes were visiting my father, they must have been fully aware of not only these dire circumstances and obstructions but also the threats and difficulties arising from the Soviet sphere of influence that was gaining hold in Czechoslovakia. (Recall that Ludik was to be denied a passport.) The Soviets were beginning to dominate plans and strategies for reconstruction. Russia was gaining control over key ministries and thus was able to suppress non-communist activity. Thoughts of a more equitable distribution of power were quickly disappearing, and President Edward Benes's dream that the country could become a bridge between the East and the West were being dashed. By February 1948, the communists had seized full power in a coup d'état. And that is when all visits to our house came to an end.

During the period (1953) when my family and I were being benignly questioned by some career bureaucrat in order that we might enter the United States, the fate of those who had worked for the USC in Czechoslovakia was tragic, horrible, and torturously protracted. Gejza Pavlik and Noel Field, among many others, were being subjected to brutal investigations, house arrest, prison, and Cold War show trials, held in Eastern Europe, in which they were charged with serving the interests of Western imperialism. Field was also accused, by the FBI, of feeding information to the Soviets. For this reason, in October, 1947, he was fired from his position with the USC, and his papers in the USC files "sanitized." Field was never able to return to America and was eventually granted political asylum in Budapest. Throughout, he never let go of his belief in pacifism, egalitarianism, and human service. To the last, he clung to an idealism that the historian Arthur Schlesinger, Jr. called both "simple-minded and indestructible."

Pavlik, though not as well known, suffered from brutal investigation methods in Hungary. Labeling him a Trotskyite, an enemy, a spy, the Soviets poured strong salt solutions down his throat, beat him, struck the soles of his feet with rubber hoses, deprived him of sleep, and threatened him with "suicide" or "an escape attempt," during which he would be shot. At a trial in Budapest, he admitted that he had consciously decided to spy for the Americans, but he later retracted his confession. Finally, on June 29, 1950, Pavlik was sentenced to fifteen years in prison, his wife to ten. And so goes the world.

ACKNOWLEDGMENTS

With many thanks to those who have chosen to spend time reading through the manuscript. In particular, I would like to acknowledge Carrie Bramen, Regina Grol, and Carolyn Korsmeyer. I am also grateful for the encouragement I received from Kim Chinquee, Joyce Gleason, Ephraim Massey, and Phil Brodrock.

ABOUT THE AUTHOR

author photo © Bruce Fox

Ann C. Colley spent the first thirteen years of her life in England during World War II and the postwar years. In 1953, she moved with her parents to the United States. After receiving her PhD in English from the University of Chicago, she taught at Fisk University. In 1980, she moved to the State University College of New York in Buffalo where she is a SUNY Distinguished Professor.

The author has written extensively on nineteenth-century British literature and culture. She has published with such presses as Harcourt, Brace, Jovanovich, the University of Georgia Press, Macmillan, Ashgate, Palgrave, Routledge, and the Cambridge University Press. She has taught on Fulbright Fellowships in Poland and Ukraine. With Irving Massey, she has traveled throughout South America, Central America, Nepal, Turkey, Morocco, Africa, New Zealand, Armenia, Belarus, Hungary, the Soviet Union, Czechoslovakia, Poland, and Ukraine. Always longing for the landscape of home, she often returns to England. In the summers, she lives in the wilderness of Nova Scotia.

SELECTED TITLES FROM SHE WRITES PRESS

She Writes Press is an independent publishing company founded to serve women writers everywhere. Visit us at www.shewritespress.com.

Dearest Ones at Home: Clara Taylor's Letters from Russia, 1917–1919 edited by Katrina Maloney and Patricia Maloney. Clara Taylor's detailed, delightful letters documenting her two years in Russia teaching factory girls self-sufficiency skills—right in the middle of World War I.

Motherlines: Letters of Love, Longing, and Liberation by Patricia Reis. $16.95, 978-1-63152-121-8. In her midlife search for meaning, and longing for maternal connection, Patricia Reis encounters uncommon women who inspire her journey and discovers an unlikely confidante in her aunt, a free-spirited Franciscan nun.

Gap Year Girl by Marianne Bohr. $16.95, 978-1-63152-820-0. Thirty-plus years after first backpacking through Europe, Marianne Bohr and her husband leave their lives behind and take off on a yearlong quest for adventure.

The Beauty of What Remains: Family Lost, Family Found by Susan Johnson Hadler. $16.95, 978-1-63152-007-5. Susan Johnson Hadler goes on a quest to find out who the missing people in her family were—and what happened to them—and succeeds in reuniting a family shattered for four generations.

The Butterfly Groove: A Mother's Mystery, A Daughter's Journey by Jessica Barraco. $16.95, 978-1-63152-800-2. In an attempt to solve the mystery of her deceased mother's life, Jessica Barraco retraces the older woman's steps nearly forty years earlier—and finds herself along the way.

Godmother: An Unexpected Journey, Perfect Timing, and Small Miracles by Odile Atthalin. $16.95, 978-1-63152-172-0. After thirty years of traveling the world, Odile Atthalin—a French intellectual from a well-to-do family in Paris—ends up in Berkeley, CA, where synchronicities abound and ultimately give her everything she has been looking for, including the gift of becoming a godmother.

Printed in the United States
by Baker & Taylor Publisher Services